MAXIM GORKY

Born Alexei Maximovich Peshkov in 1868, Maxim Gorky was a Russian and Soviet writer and a political activist. His first novel, *Foma Gordeyev*, was published in 1899 and dedicated to Anton Chekhov, who became a cherished friend and urged Gorky to write his first play, *Philistines*, for the Moscow Art Theatre. A five-time nominee for the Nobel Prize in Literature, Gorky's best-known plays outside Russia, all premiered between 1902 and 1911, include *Summerfolk*, *Children of the Sun*, *Barbarians*, *Enemies* and *Vassa Zheleznova*. In 1906, his involvement in radical politics, and increasing identification with the Bolsheviks led him to flee Russia for New York, where he wrote his novel, *The Mother*, and then the Italian island of Capri, where he lived for seven years. He had complex relationships with both Lenin and Stalin, who persuaded Gorky to return to the Soviet Union as a permanent resident and to become his 'superindentent of writers'. Perhaps his most lasting work is the autobiographical trilogy, *My Childhood*, *My Apprenticeship* and *My Universities*. Gorky died in Moscow in 1936.

MIKE BARTLETT

Mike Bartlett is a multi-award-winning playwright and
screenwriter whose most recent plays include *Snowflake* (Old
Fire Station, Oxford/Kiln Theatre, London); *Albion* (Almeida
Theatre); *Wild* (Hampstead Theatre); *Game* (Almeida Theatre);
King Charles III (Almeida Theatre/West End/Broadway;
Critics' Circle Award for Best New Play, Olivier Award for Best
New Play, Tony Nomination for Best Play); *An Intervention*
(Paines Plough/Watford Palace Theatre); *Bull* (Sheffield
Theatres/Off-Broadway; TMA Best New Play Award, Olivier
Award for Outstanding Achievement in an Affiliate Theatre);
Medea (Glasgow Citizens/Headlong); *Chariots of Fire* (based
on the film; Hampstead/West End); *13* (National Theatre); *Love,
Love, Love* (Paines Plough/Plymouth Drum/Royal Court
Theatre; TMA Best New Play Award); *Earthquakes in London*
(Headlong/National Theatre); *Cock* (Royal Court/Off-
Broadway, Olivier Award for Outstanding Achievement in an
Affiliate Theatre); *Artefacts* (nabokov/Bush Theatre);
Contractions and *My Child* (Royal Court).

Bartlett has also written several plays for radio, winning the
Writers' Guild Tinniswood and Imison Prizes for *Not Talking*.
He has received BAFTA nominations for his television series
The Town and *Doctor Foster* for which Bartlett won
Outstanding Newcomer for British Television Writing at the
British Screenwriters' Awards 2016. Bartlett's adaptation of his
play *King Charles III* aired on BBC television in 2017.

Maxim Gorky

VASSA

in a new version by
Mike Bartlett

NICK HERN BOOKS
London
www.nickhernbooks.co.uk

A Nick Hern Book

This version of *Vassa* first published in Great Britain in 2019 as a paperback original by Nick Hern Books Limited, The Glasshouse, 49a Goldhawk Road, London W12 8QP

This version of *Vassa* copyright © 2019 Mike Bartlett

Mike Bartlett has asserted his right to be identified as the author of this version

Cover artwork by Nadav Kander

Designed and typeset by Nick Hern Books, London
Printed in Great Britain by Mimeo Ltd, Huntingdon, Cambridgeshire PE29 6XX

A CIP catalogue record for this book is available from the British Library

ISBN 978 1 84842 916 1

Woodland
CARBON
www.woodlandcarbon.co.uk
NICK HERN BOOKS
Printed on Carbon Captured paper

Vassa was first performed at the Almeida Theatre, London, on 21 October 2019 (previews from 9 October), with the following cast:

LIPA	Alexandra Dowling
PROKHOR	Michael Gould
PAVEL	Arthur Hughes
DUNYA	Daniella Isaacs
ANNA	Amber James
SEMYON	Danny Kirrane
NATALYA	Kayla Meikle
MIKHAIL	Cyril Nri
VASSA	Siobhán Redmond
LYUDMILA	Sophie Wu

Direction	Tinuke Craig
Design	Fly Davis
Light	Joshua Pharo
Sound	Emma Laxton
Movement	Jenny Ogilvie
Casting	Annelie Powell CDG
Resident Director	Tamar Saphra

Characters

VASSA PETROVNA ZHELEZNOVA
ANNA
SEMYON } *her children*
PAVEL
NATALYA, *Semyon's wife*
LYUDMILA, *Pavel's wife*
PROKHOR ZHELEZNOV, *Zakhar's brother*
MIKHAILO VASILIEV, *manager*
DUNYECHKA, *a distant relative of the Zheleznovs*
LIPA, *a maid*

(/) *means the next speech begins at that point.*
(–) *means the next line interrupts.*
(…) *at the end of a speech means it trails off. On its own it indicates a pressure, expectation or desire to speak.*

This text went to press before the end of rehearsals and so may differ slightly from the play as performed.

As the audience enters, Russian music from before the Revolution is playing.

Just before house lights go down we hear the opening of The Firebird *'Suite 1. Introduction'.*

As it plays, the house lights slowly fade.

A caption:

'This play is set before a revolution.'

It fades. Then another caption.

'Capitalism is showing its age.'

It fades.

ACT ONE

*Early morning, a winter's day. A large room – VASSA
ZHELEZNOVA's bedroom and study. It is crowded with things.
In the corner behind screens is a bed, to the left is a table,
covered in papers, with tiles used instead of paperweights. By the
table is a tall writing desk, behind that, under the window, is
a couch. There are lamps with green lampshades. In the right-
hand corner there is a tiled stove-bench, and by that is a safe and
a door leading into the chapel. Papers are pinned to the screens
with safety pins, they rustle when anyone walks past them.*

*In the upstage wall there are wide doors leading into the dining
room; a table can be seen, and above it a chandelier. A candle
is burning on the table. DUNYA is getting the breakfast things
ready. LIPA carries in a boiling samovar.*

DUNYA	(*Quietly.*) Is she back yet?
LIPA	No.
DUNYA	So what's going to happen?
LIPA	Er. Shut up?
	LIPA enters VASSA's room and inspects it.
	VASSA enters through the doors to the chapel, adjusting her glasses and the hair at her temples.
VASSA	You're incredibly late.
LIPA	No, I –
VASSA	It's quarter past seven.
LIPA	No it's not –
VASSA	'No'?
	VASSA picks up the clock and shows her.
	Look.

LIPA   Alright. I'm sorry.

VASSA   *Look.*

            She does.

            You can read a clock?

LIPA   Yes I can read a clock.

VASSA   What time is it then?

LIPA   I was talking to –

VASSA   (*Very calm.*) What time is it Lipa?

            She looks.

LIPA   Quarter past seven.

VASSA   At last.

LIPA   If you'll let me speak, Vassa, I was getting up to
            date with everything this morning. Zakhar
            Ivanovich was bad again last night.

VASSA   (*Going to the table.*) Hm. No telegram?

LIPA   No.

VASSA   And everyone's up?

LIPA   Pavel hasn't gone to bed yet...

VASSA   Why not? Is he ill?

LIPA   No it's because Lyudmila spent the night with
            someone else I mean with somewhere else I mean
            she wasn't at home last night and I'm not saying
            anything but I don't know what she was doing.

            A moment. VASSA *approaches* LIPA, *calmly.*
            Speaks quietly.

VASSA   Lipa I think your time with us is coming to an end.

LIPA   (*Frightened.*) What? Why? What have I done?

VASSA   You tell me bad news with a little smile on your
            face. You can't help it. You *enjoy* it.

LIPA   No, I don't.

VASSA   You realise if I *did* let you go, people would
              know what you were like because I would tell
              them, so you wouldn't get any other work and
              you'd quickly be out in the street, either having
              sex with fat men for money or more likely
              starving to death lying in some gutter being
              chewed on by rats, torn into pieces and then the
              rain would just carry away the you-sludge
              forever, down down into the sewer –

LIPA   I was just –

VASSA   – so be careful, cos I'm your best bet. I might
              seem cruel but considering what you deserve, I'm
              a saint.

LIPA   Yes Vassa Petrovna.

VASSA   Now go and call everyone for breakfast. Dunya!
              Cup! Lipa stop! If Lyudmila is still asleep, don't
              wake her, and if anyone asks, she spent last night
              with her father.

LIPA   Her father? But she didn't – she – Oh you mean
              lie –

VASSA   – and send him in to see me.

LIPA   (*Quietly as she goes.*) With her *father.* Okay good
              luck / with that…

DUNYA   (*Carrying in the tea.*) Morning Vassa.

VASSA   Has he died yet?

DUNYA   No. But he was so ill last night, he was sick in
              a shoe.

VASSA   Whose shoe?

DUNYA   Well he started in his own but I thought that
              wasn't right so I offered him mine.

VASSA   Has he said anything?

DUNYA   No. To be honest I'm not sure he will, ever again.
             I mean, he's just... blinking.

             Like...

             She demonstrates blinking.

VASSA   Yes alright. Go and listen to what they say about
             Lyudmila, then come back and tell me. Go on go
             to the table.

             Exit DUNYA. VASSA *lifts her glasses to her
             forehead, moving her lips.* MIKHAIL *enters.*

MIKHAIL   Vassa Petrovna a very good / morning to –

VASSA   Mikhail, can't you control your daughter?

MIKHAIL   I'm afraid not. Lyudmila is a law to herself.
             Whenever I try to talk to her, she just rolls her
             eyes and is like 'yeah okay Dad'. She says my
             voice is really boring. That it doesn't modulate in
             tone enough. Which might be true but it is what
             it is –

VASSA   She stayed at yours last night.

MIKHAIL   No we don't know where she was she – oh, I see,
             yes *at mine*, good.

VASSA   And I don't like to give parenting advice but if
             she really won't listen to you Mikhail, slap her.

MIKHAIL   ...slap her...?

VASSA   Just once. But quite hard. Yes? A shock. Show
             her who's in charge.

MIKHAIL   But Vassa... I...

VASSA   Or grab her by the hair. That works. Fling her
             about a bit.

             MIKHAIL *smiles.*

             I'm not joking. It's what she needs. I'll do it if
             you can't. I hear Zakhar's bad?

MIKHAIL	Yes.
VASSA	He couldn't sign the will?
MIKHAIL	No.
VASSA	But did the priest agree to witness anyway?
MIKHAIL	I'm afraid the priest is asking for three hundred.
VASSA	Three...?!
	Fine. Do it. Fuck it. Hope he enjoys it. The others are all...?
MIKHAIL	The others are fine, it's just the priest.
VASSA	Get his signature on the will today. And when that's done we'll think how to deal with the children...
MIKHAIL	Yes we'll have to.
VASSA	Why won't Anna come? There's no telegram... I thought there would be by now – Dunya, where's my fucking *cup*!
	She hears a noise from the dining room.
	Who's in there?
PAVEL	(*In the dining room.*) Me...
VASSA	Why are you hiding?
	PAVEL *enters, pretending to be proud.*
PAVEL	(*Enters.*) I'm not hiding. I'm simply / arriving for breakfast –
VASSA	You should say hello to your mother in the morning.
PAVEL	Good morning Mother.
	He sees MIKHAIL.
	Oh. Where's your daughter?

MIKHAIL   Your wife you mean. No idea. She's your
           responsibility. I handed her over at the wedding.

VASSA   You can go Mikhail.

           He does. Once he's left, PAVEL *collapses in
           torment.*

PAVEL   Oh God Mum, it's awful. Everyone knows.
           They're looking at me weirdly, like I'm some
           kind of freak.

VASSA   Surely you're used to that.

PAVEL   No – I mean because of what's *happened*!!
           God!... it's so shit, my wife has just gone! Mum
           please, I'm not strong enough for this.

VASSA   I said at the time she wasn't a good match. You
           should have married someone... well... like you.

PAVEL   Ugly.

VASSA   No! *Quiet,* I was going to say, but yes alright,
           I mean there's certainly an aesthetic *gap* between
           the two of you –

PAVEL   Right I'm ugly so I should have an ugly wife. So
           there could be two of us, staggering around,
           couple of crips together –

           As he does an impression of this, VASSA
           extinguishes the candle then turns to him.

VASSA   Do you want them to laugh at you or feel sorry
           for you?

PAVEL   *Neither.*

VASSA   Then stop moaning. Right now.

PAVEL   But it's *shameful* –

           Unseen by PAVEL, MIKHAIL *comes back in,
           and picks up his glasses that he left behind.*

– the wife of a Zheleznov turns out to be a total fucking *slut*!

PAVEL *sees him.*

No offence.

MIKHAIL   I left my glasses.

He goes again. VASSA *turns to* PAVEL.

VASSA   Go and have breakfast.

She goes into the dining room. Speaks to DUNYA –

Why haven't you put the candle out, you weird monastic crow?

PAVEL   Mum, please, I need some money. I'm going into town… I can't be here…

VASSA   You… Your father is critically ill, and you want to go to town? Anything else you want to do? Have a party in his room? Why not take him dancing? He can't move that much I'm told, but apparently he can still *blink*, so that's something. You're 'going to town'? Brilliant. What a characteristically thick idea.

A moment. PAVEL, *upset.*

PAVEL   Well what *should I do*?!

He throws himself onto the couch, weeping furiously.

VASSA *rolls her eyes and turns to go into the dining room.*

VASSA   Don't ruin my cushions…

In the dining room, NATALYA *walks over to her mother-in-law, kisses her hand.*

Did you sleep in?

NATALYA   I was up with your husband until three o'clock.

VASSA   I'm told he was bad.

NATALYA   Yes. He was sick in Dunya's shoe.

            PAVEL *cries*.

            Who's crying? Have you been mean to Lipa
            again?

VASSA   No, it's a seven-year-old girl.

            NATALYA *goes to investigate*. VASSA *drinks
            tea*.

            She just came in and started screaming so I –

NATALYA   (*Going into the study*.) Pavel! Oh… What are you
            doing? Dunya, get some water!

VASSA   Oh, come on, don't overdo it, he doesn't…

            DUNYA *enters and looks around*.

            Well, what have you been told? Get some
            water…

            DUNYA *goes off*. VASSA *comes back into the
            living room*.

            Pavel, I'm sorry.

PAVEL   You're not.

VASSA   No, I am. I should have hidden you away
            somewhere a long time ago.

PAVEL   Yes! Exactly! You're not ashamed *for* me, you're
            ashamed *of* me.

VASSA   Yes but that's only natural, I mean look at you.

NATALYA   You're a man Pavel, you shouldn't cry.

PAVEL   Don't *touch* me… I make your skin crawl, you
            think I'm a total failure.

            MIKHAIL *enters the dining room, tugging at his
            moustache, anxious*.

Because my wife, Lyudmila Zheleznova, is the biggest fucking *whore* on the entire *planet*!

MIKHAIL *stops. Offended.* PAVEL *sees him.*

Oh… Perfect.

He leaves. NATALYA *goes after him.*

VASSA   What's wrong?

DUNYA *comes in with a large pot of water.*

MIKHAIL   (*Entering her room.*) May I come in?

VASSA   Yes, of course. Dunya, what are you doing? Go away.

DUNYA *looks confused. Dumps the pot and leaves.*

MIKHAIL   Lyudmila has left with Prokhor.

VASSA   Prokhor? Right. Alright… Where to?

MIKHAIL   The village…

VASSA   She – Oh! The *village*! I thought you meant for *good*. Oh well the village, that's not so bad. You frightened me. Does Pavel know?

MIKHAIL   He will. So my only daughter is lost…

And the business, *your* business, that I have dedicated my whole life to, is collapsing!

VASSA   (*Annoyed.*) Errrr – no it's not. Stop moaning. *Shush*. It's fine. Your daughter slept with my brother-in-law. Her uncle technically. And that's not *great*, but on the positive side he's not her uncle by *blood*, that would be much worse –

MIKHAIL   He's an enemy to everyone.

VASSA   And the business is *not* collapsing, actually, Mikhail, not yet. Lots to do.

MIKHAIL   (*In a rage.*) You walk around and everyone thinks of Prokhor as so *good*. Salt of the earth, human

being. *Conscientious*, they say... well in
business, men like that, they're like sand in
a machine, you know what I mean? They break
the whole thing. And it's all just pretend anyway
– 'goodness'. Give me what I'm worth, nothing
more. You can keep *love*. *Jokes*. And when
someone doesn't have anything to offer of any
real interest, he pretends he has a conscience!
And that makes everyone around him *feel* for him
and *agree* and *cry*... and suddenly you can't work
properly any more...

VASSA   So what are you going to do?

MIKHAIL   What?

VASSA   Get revenge or something? Get back at him? It's
              okay. You can tell me.

              Beat.

MIKHAIL   Well... I'll... wait a bit... probably.

VASSA   I see. You're going to wait. What a guy.

MIKHAIL   You should go to Zakhar.

VASSA   I know I know – There's still no telegram from
              Anna?

MIKHAIL   What are you hoping for? She's not going to
              come. She's got a whole other life.

VASSA   (*Leaving.*) Yes alright. Enough. Come with me
              but don't talk.

              He does and they exit.

              DUNYA *appears noiselessly, sits at the table,
              crosses herself and whispers.*

DUNYA   Oh Lord, save and pardon your servants at every
              step on their journey...

              LIPA *runs in.*

LIPA   Where's Vassa? She's here!

DUNYA   Anna?

LIPA   Lyudmila! She went off with her Prokhor last night. Her *uncle*! It's like a huge thing. Didn't you know?

SEMYON enters.

SEMYON   Know what? What's going on?! Intrigue?! I *love* intrigue! Well?

LIPA   Oh. Er. Nothing.

She goes.

SEMYON   'Er' – 'Er' – Stupid wench. Yes, what? Go on Dunya. *Pour.*

DUNYA pours some tea.

How's my father?

DUNYA   Not well... I think he's close to the end now.

SEMYON   Believe it when I see it.

He yawns.

Has everyone had breakfast?

DUNYA   (*Half-whispering.*) Not Pavel. He hasn't touched anything.

His wife wasn't home last night...

SEMYON   (*Pleasantly surprised.*) Reall-lly?

DUNYA   She was with Prokhor.

SEMYON   She... No way! Ah, Uncle, randy old shit. He did it in the end. Excellent!

Ha! Look at you!

DUNYA   What?

SEMYON   Your eyebrows.

DUNYA   Well it's *shameful*.

SEMYON laughs.

SEMYON   I know! It's awful! Ah! The face Pavel must be
            pulling right now. Hilarious. Prokhor!

PROKHOR   (*Entering, muttering.*) I'll rip his fucking ears
            off –

SEMYON   Whose ears?

PROKHOR   Who's do you think?! The freak's. The hunchback
            of notre-cock... He's let Rigoletto into the
            dovecot again...

SEMYON   Who's Rigoletto?

PROKHOR   Rigoletto.

            Rigoletto. Without the leg.

            Stumpy Rigoletto.

            Pegoletto.

SEMYON   I don't –

PROKHOR   The *cat*! My hands are shaking I'm so angry,
            look!

SEMYON   Right yes that explains the hands but why are
            your eyes red?

            And why are you so generally crumpled and a bit
            smelly?

PROKHOR   What?

SEMYON   Did you sleep in your clothes?

PROKHOR   (*Examining himself.*) Me? Oh. Shit. You're right
            I look like a laundry basket.

SEMYON   At best.

PROKHOR   I should get changed. Pig! Where's breakfast?
            Agh, Pavel's such a collosal penis. That fucking
            cat strangled Skobarya and two black-piebald
            pigeons.

SEMYON   He did it deliberately?

PROKHOR   The cat?

SEMYON   *Pavel*, letting the cat / in –

PROKHOR   Of course he did it / deliberately.

SEMYON   But why would he, Uncle? What on *earth* would make him so angry?

           A moment. SEMYON *grinning at* PROKHOR.

PROKHOR   Semyon you know where the line is. Don't *cross it*. That woman should be an actress or something… a model! She's not just in a different league to him, she's practically a separate species.

           LIPA *enters*.

LIPA   Prokhor Ivanovich…

PROKHOR   What?

LIPA   The Manager is asking for you…

PROKHOR   I am your manager, and no one else. Why are you here?

LIPA   Just… to… tell you that Mikhail, the Manager is / asking

PROKHOR   You always skulk around… you little… cockroach.

SEMYON   What does he want?

LIPA   He's… I don't know any other way to put it –

           As if to a child.

           He's ASKING. TO. SEE. / PROKHOR.

PROKHOR   See me? Impossible. I'm invisible. Tell him that he is intellectually subnormal and a criminal.

SEMYON   (*Laughing.*) Can criminals be intellectually subnormal?

PROKHOR   Of course! Have you seen our politicians?

SEMYON   I love it when you get annoyed, it's very funny.

PROKHOR. You know you could easily be a politician
Semyon.

SEMYON   You think? Yes, I've often thought perhaps
I should stand for some kind of office. I tend to
be a natural leader in any situation –

LYUDMILA *enters in a dressing gown. She
speaks to* LIPA *without looking at her.*

LYUDMILA Milk.

LIPA *goes.*

DUNYA *bows silently,* PROKHOR *twirls his
moustache and grunts,* SEMYON*'s grinning.*

Don't smile at me.

SEMYON   All nature smiles when it sees you.

SEMYON *laughs.*

LYUDMILA (*To* DUNYA.) You see? One of his parents is
about to die and he is laughing like a fucking
hyena.

SEMYON *quickly becomes serious.*

Dunya you should teach him some decency –

DUNYA   Yes...

SEMYON   (*In a tone of self-justification.*) My father has
been at death's door for seven months now –

PROKHOR I know and he's generally such a decisive person.

DUNYA   (*Involuntarily.*) Oh, Lord...

PROKHOR What?

DUNYA   Just, the way you all –

LYUDMILA (*To* DUNYA.) Go then.

DUNYA   Where?

LYUDMILA Wherever you have to. Uncle Prokhor is severely
immoral, and it's not right for a decent woman

like you to be in the same room. God knows what he might do to you. Even with his eyes. He's probably undressing you right now.

DUNYA *goes*.

I don't like spies. (*To* PROKHOR.) Listen, you Spaniard –

SEMYON   Ah! Spaniard! Yes! He's / just like one! Ha!

LYUDMILA I'm going to bed. I'll get up at four – you'll be ready then. Alright?

PROKHOR   Alright.

SEMYON   The two of you going for a ride?

A pause. LYUDMILA *and* PROKHOR *just look at* SEMYON.

LYUDMILA In the troika, yes.

SEMYON   Really?!

PROKHOR   Absolutely. Do you want to come with us? Bring your wife if you like? We could all ride together.

LYUDMILA *Stop it*.

SEMYON   (*Scratches himself, sadly.*) Ah, well my wife gets travel sick unfortunately.

And there's Pavel to think about.

LYUDMILA What about Pavel?

SEMYON   Well... it's awkward isn't it?

LYUDMILA Why?

SEMYON   Well... You know...

SEMYON *laughs embarrassedly*, PROKHOR *watches him, shaking his head hopelessly*.

VASSA *enters*.

VASSA   Semyon, go into the study.

He does. VASSA *turns to* LYUDMILA.

Hello sweetheart. Have we seen each other yet this morning?

LYUDMILA   No.

VASSA   Then why aren't you saying hello?

LYUDMILA   (*Affectionately.*) Of course. Sorry.

She hauls herself to her feet and heads towards VASSA.

PROKHOR   (*Gets up.*) Attentshun!

Just as LYUDMILA *goes in to kiss* VASSA, VASSA *grabs her, firmly, calmly, sternly. Speaks quietly.*

VASSA   What the hell do you think you're doing?

LYUDMILA*'s shocked – and in close proximity to* VASSA, *scared.*

LYUDMILA   I... don't know... honestly!

VASSA   You don't know.

LYUDMILA   No. I... I... sorry – I really –

Upset, she quickly leaves.

PROKHOR   Boom! Dead! Ha! Love that!

VASSA   (*Softly, peaceably.*) Prokhor, you're a clever man.

PROKHOR   I know.

VASSA   Clever enough to know that your actions are an embarrassment to the whole household. You're putting our long-standing business affairs in a shameful light...

PROKHOR   That's almost word for word the same lecture I've heard from my brother.

VASSA   I know. Zakhar always tried. But it never made any difference, did it?

PROKHOR   As I said to him, it's too late to teach this old dog anything new. I live my life!

VASSA   Then what about that girl? She has a life to live too –

PROKHOR   She's an adult. Knows what she's doing.

VASSA   I thought she did but she's run off with *you*, which seems... well... no offence but... unlikely.

PROKHOR   Excuse me! I understand a good deal more than you about young women... as well as seeing right through many women of a more... mature age...

VASSA   Fine you don't care about her, then what about Pavel? He's your nephew.

PROKHOR   Ah, Pavel, yes, can you be so kind as to tell him if he's going to destroy my pigeons with his cats, I will rip his ears off the side of his head, I will actually, literally do that.

VASSA   You want to go against us. My family.

PROKHOR   Family?!! Vassa, in case you've forgotten, with your help my brother nearly ruined my business and would've seen me out onto the street. 'Family'?! Family ripped me off by thirty thousand –

VASSA   (*Quietly.*) You want a fight?

PROKHOR   Sure. Who with?

VASSA   With your nephews, I imagine...

PROKHOR   Let's stop this. There won't be any fights. There's a law, Vassa. A proper Roman, Russian, big shiny massive fucking *law*. What's mine is mine! Zakhar will shortly go up to the great market in the sky and forty days later I shall take from the business my share, with no shouting, no fights. All done.

            Good day to you...

            He quickly exits.

            VASSA *watches him go, strangely bowed, as if she wants to spring at him.*

Enter NATALYA, *sits at the table, pours herself some tea.*

VASSA   (*Blankly.*) How's Pavel?

NATALYA   He's calmed down a bit...

Silence. VASSA *paces around the dining room.*

I feel sorry for him.

VASSA   What? Why don't you speak properly?

NATALYA   I speak completely normally you just don't –

VASSA   *What?*

NATALYA   I *said* I feel I sorry for Pavel.

VASSA   No one's ever felt sorry for me. When Zakhar started going bankrupt, I was six months' pregnant with Pavel. Everything smelt of prison. Police. At that time we were secretly pawnbrokers, you know what a / pawnbroker is?

NATALYA   Yes of course I / know what a pawnbroker is –

VASSA   We had chests filled with other people's things, we had to hide it, cover everything. I said Zakhar! Let me give birth! And he screamed at me to shut up and carry on. So I did I carried on, fumbling around in terror... no help, no salvation for another two months and then... eventually this child arrived in the middle of it all.

NATALYA   Maybe that's why he was born like that.

VASSA   He was five when I noticed... but yes... exactly.

Anyway that was just the start of all this shit.

NATALYA   Everyone swears a lot in this house.

VASSA   We're passionate.

Beat.

NATALYA   Did you talk to that cutter you got rid of the other day?

VASSA	No. About what? He was useless.
NATALYA	But did you talk to him about life?
VASSA	Life? Whose life?
NATALYA	All life... everybody's.
VASSA	Er, no, actually. As I fired him it didn't occur to me to ask about his views on 'all life'. Why would I –
NATALYA	Because he said all business was a sin.
VASSA	Did he? Idiot.
NATALYA	Why is that so stupid? You criticise everyone for –
VASSA	Business a sin? Is work a sin? What excuses people make up to justify sitting around. There was this... homeless person, a tramp, basically, this was before your time... he used to come round, park himself in the kitchen and give sermons exactly like that. His name was Ivan. He said that all work done with human hands is sinful. So I said, 'Alright then, Ivan, put that bread down, don't eat it, it's made by hand. Don't *sin*.' Then I had him thrown out. No one heard from him again. Without business. Without work. Without sin.

And dead, now, probably. |
NATALYA	Just saying maybe he had a –
	VASSA*'s not listening, she goes to ring the bell.*
	Oh, no, not listening again / what a surprise –
VASSA	People overcomplicate everything. Zakhar didn't, he came from the poorest family and look where he got.
NATALYA	Dying a horrible death.
VASSA	But at least he lived!

NATALYA   You were always complaining about him...

VASSA   Well that's what women *do*! Complain. All the
time, if we're honest. And it makes sense. If
you're not allowed to do what you want, it's all
we've got left. But I don't blame him for living.
I'd have done the same if I could. He slept
around his whole life, had a fabulous fucking
time, and now he's dying from it. There you go.
But he was great value, in so many ways. My
promiscuous, sucessful, overbearing husband.
I can't praise him enough.

    LIPA *enters*. NATALYA *leaves – as she does –*

NATALYA   You say one thing, then something completely
different.

VASSA   (*To herself, quietly.*) And that's the fun...

    Once NATALYA*'s left,* VASSA *turns to* LIPA.

    So who was at Prokhor's yesterday evening?

LIPA   Someone called Evgenii Mironich... I think he's
a lawyer or something.

VASSA   Yes, from town... don't you know him?

LIPA   I can't afford lawyers.

VASSA   What did they talk about?

LIPA   I didn't hear.

VASSA   Why not?

LIPA   They locked themselves in.

VASSA   What about the vent in the stove? You normally –

LIPA   They were too quiet.

    VASSA *looks at her.*

VASSA   I gave you simple instructions.

LIPA   Yes – Vassa I tried.

VASSA   Remember what you are. What you've done.

LIPA   I know, I know, if people had any idea I would go to a nunnery...

VASSA   Nunnery?! Ha! Oh that's sweet, but I doubt they'd have you Lipa.

LIPA tries to be strong but starts crying –

Oh... oh no, please – don't –

LIPA gets her handkerchief out.

But carries on crying.

Really snotty crying.

Jesus, wipe it off.

LIPA tries.

No. It's still...

She tries again. The snotty crying is very noisy and disgusting.

How is there so much?

She keeps trying, but she's still crying.

No there's still a bit.

She keeps doing it, badly, and noisily. Eventually –

Here.

VASSA grabs the handkerchief violently, making LIPA flinch but then she carefully, almost tenderly, wipes LIPA's face.

No, my Lipa, if I let you go, it wouldn't be a nunnery. It would be rats.

She's finished.

There. Call Mikhail.

VASSA *sees* PAVEL *lurking.*

What are you doing Pavel?

PAVEL   (*In the doorway.*) Nothing·

VASSA   (*To* LIPA.) *Go.*

LIPA *goes.* VASSA *turns to* PAVEL.

Nothing. What does that mean? Where does this come from? This laziness. Just... hanging around...

PAVEL   Well what should I do?! There's nowhere for me to go. My *heart is dying...*

VASSA   Jesus Pavel your wife *loves sex.* Just unfortunately not with you. Which is fair enough, if we're honest, isn't it, given...

And the truth is, if you can't control her you'll just have to put up with it until the time comes...

PAVEL   What time? You mean... Mum, you're so cruel sometimes. You'd dig the earth with me like a spade, if you could get money from it –

VASSA   A... What on earth does that mean?

Wait – A nunnery...??

She turns to PAVEL.

Yes! Pavel! You should go to a monastery.

PAVEL   A... monastery? Me? Why?

VASSA   Well you're right, with the way you are, and your wife having all this sex with your uncle, where else can you go?

PAVEL   Are you serious?

VASSA   Completely.

PAVEL   (*In a rage.*) But... you... you can't. You won't. Look at you... Look at you!

He backs away, out of the room.

I'm not scared of you, I'm not scared...

He goes.

VASSA *goes into the study, sits at the table and goes through her papers, bringing them up to her face, her hands are shaking.*

She's muttering to herself but we can't hear her...

She throws down the papers, takes her glasses and sits without moving, sternly, sadly looking out.

MIKHAIL *enters, full of spite and anger.*

MIKHAIL	Yes Vassa? You sent for me? How can I help?
VASSA	What's the tone?
MIKHAIL	What?
VASSA	Your daughter is right about your voice, normally it's pretty monotonous, but something's happened. You're angry aren't you?
MIKHAIL	No. I –
VASSA	With me?
MIKHAIL	No I just – they wear me down... Semyon keeps on laughing –
VASSA	Shush. Moaning. Did you know that there was a lawyer at Prokhor's last night?
MIKHAIL	Yes... But why?

VASSA *shrugs.*

That Lipa of yours... you sent her to listen.

VASSA	Yes but she didn't manage it. She's forgotten to be frightened recently. We need to bring the *terror* back. She's even smirking.
MIKHAIL	She killed her *child*. If you were to tell anyone –

VASSA   If I was to tell anyone it's dangerous for us too.
             Which maybe she's counting on.

MIKHAIL   I don't see why it's dangerous for us?

VASSA   Well it was Semyon's.

MIKHAIL   Yes but there's no proof! Children don't come
             labelled, thank god. When it arrives, it's just
             a child with a mother. The father's forever a
             mystery if he wants to be. That's natural. How it
             should be. At least that won't ever change.

VASSA   Talk to her. It's better coming from a man.
             Frighten her, then immediately be nice to her…
             That normally does it.

MIKHAIL   Right. Yes I can do that.

             A moment.

VASSA   I spoke to Prokhor. He said he'll ruin me.

MIKHAIL   Well he might!

             VASSA *looks down, thinking.*

             Perhaps it's time for serious measures…

             She doesn't look at him.

VASSA   Like what?

MIKHAIL   Prokhor's heart is weak.

VASSA   Is it?

MIKHAIL   Yes. And people like that often die, suddenly.

VASSA   Rubbish! He'll outlive both of us.

MIKHAIL   Yes if we leave it to God. But he takes this
             medicine, more and more. I know from the
             chemist's bill. Yakov Fershal said that the
             medicines he's taking, they can be dangerous…

VASSA   Yakov Fershal gets drunk and lies…

MIKHAIL   There are two apparently. One is for the heart, and the other – well – I don't how to say this – it's for –

VASSA   For his cock.

MIKHAIL   His… yes. And Yakov Fershal is afraid –

VASSA   Yakov Fershal isn't qualified in anything –

MIKHAIL   – he says that if taken the wrong way, the mixtures could work against each other. If you increased the dose…

VASSA   I once saw Yakov Fershal trip over his own arm.

MIKHAIL   Vassa –

VASSA   An alcoholic gives you a medical opinion and you listen. Go and talk to Lipa.

MIKHAIL   I will, but I'm just saying it's urgent! If Zakhar was to die right now, before things were –

VASSA   It's almost as if you are suggesting we should deliberately poison Prokhor.

With his two medicines.

It's almost like that's what you're suggesting openly to me.

Which would be a stupid thing to do.

Wouldn't it?

Given the constant listening that goes on.

A pause. The penny drops.

MIKHAIL   Oh! For heaven's sake! What do you mean? Poison?! I hadn't even thought of that!

VASSA   Be more careful…

MIKHAIL   Ffu– you scared me. I mean it's offensive actually to think that I, of all people, would be suggesting something like *that*!

She looks at him a moment.

VASSA   Mikhail. You're the only person that makes me feel calm… Lyudmila might not appreciate the relentless monotony of your voice. But I find it strangely soothing. So please, stay as boring as possible.

MIKHAIL   For you Vassa. Always.

MIKHAIL *considers, then moves closer to* VASSA.

I've served you my whole life… every moment. Even my daughter… my only child… comes second to you…

He's a bit too close now…

VASSA   Yes… well, lovely, thank you, but that's probably enough. We're still holding on, thank god. And by the way, don't blame me for Lyudmila. I was against the marriage.

MIKHAIL   I know. It was Prokhor's plan, and I knew full well what he was up to. He was afraid to make Lyudmila his lover so he married her off to his nephew…

VASSA   Don't put off talking to Lipa.

MIKHAIL   I'll do it now.

VASSA   Calm yourself down, before you do.

MIKHAIL   Yes, I didn't used to get so worked up.

VASSA   And about that will, make sure the priest does what he promised.

MIKHAIL *bows respectfully, kisses her hand.*

MIKHAIL   Of course. I'll do whatever I can.

VASSA   Ah. Much better. Back to boring.

She kisses his forehead. He exits, straightening up like a soldier; following him with her gaze,

VASSA *again sits at the table, muttering indistinctly, sorting through her papers.*

ANNA *enters cautiously, looks at her mother, at first scornfully, but soon her face softens and becomes gentle, and sad.*

ANNA   Alone, just like you always used to be...

VASSA *looks up at her.*

VASSA   Anna...? Oh thank god! You're here!

ANNA   My little old mother.

VASSA   Er – Not so old –

ANNA   Hello!

VASSA   And not little actually. Just Mother is fine.

ANNA   How's Dad?

VASSA   Not good... Have you seen anyone?

ANNA   Oh just some boy who opened the door then ran away... didn't even ask who I was...

VASSA   That's Mitka, from the office... he's useless but he's cheap. Wait – I'll close the door. We should talk alone...

          Look at you, a military wife... very nice.

          She closes the door; then anxiously takes her daughter by the hand, sits on the couch.

          So, Anna...

ANNA   Yes, tell me about Dad. How is he?

VASSA   Dad? He'll never get up again. He's done. That's not the issue.

          She adopts a businesslike tone.

          Listen, there's problems. Uncle Prokhor wants to take his money out of the business and the moment your father dies, he'll be able to. But who got him that money? Who worked to support him? Zakhar and me! And what has he done to repay us? Got drunk. Chased women, and taken them to the theatre... the fucking *theatre*?!

I mean what does he want money for? He's on his own. So we have to do something! Fast.

ANNA   (*Frowning.*) Hang on...

VASSA   No, this is important. Semyon's under his wife's thumb, she's pious and awful. And trying to persuade him to take his inheritance out. Pavel's unhappy, because apparently Lyudmila's started to sleep around, which I'm not sure I understand I mean she always seemed so, you know, *frigid* to me but anyway I need help Anna! That's why I wrote to you. You're the most like me, you might look at things afresh and know what to do... at least to help with the debt.

ANNA   Debt?

VASSA   Yes there's a lot of debt as well.

ANNA   Are we ruined?

VASSA   Very nearly. Thirty years of work – everything up in smoke more or less. There are no workers, but so many worthless, lazy people looking to inherit. Why did your father and I put in all those hours? It took us years to create, and it's collapsing in days... it's unbearable. Help me!

ANNA   Has Father made a will?

Beat.

VASSA   A... will? No... I don't know...

ANNA   You don't know? You must.

VASSA   Well yes, maybe, yes he probably has... But think about it Anna – a business like this, collapsing! So talk with your brothers... they don't trust me.

They think that I want to take everything. But
you're in a good position – you have no interest
any more. You had your share of the inheritance…
when your father threw you out.

ANNA   (*Gets up.*) My *share*? Mum I was thrown ten
thousand like a beggar. That was it.

VASSA   (*Mocking smile.*) Well whatever you feel about it
we have a signed contract that says you happily
received your full share / so legally –

ANNA   (*Tenderly.*) I'd love to have that contract.

VASSA *looks at* ANNA. *Understands.*

VASSA   You are like me.

You want the contract.

ANNA   Yes please.

VASSA   If you help me.

Beat.

ANNA   Fine. But I would need you to tell me everything.

VASSA   Not a problem.

ANNA *starts to walk away.* VASSA *follows.*

How are you?

ANNA   (*Reluctantly.*) Good.

VASSA   Your husband?

ANNA   Promoted to Lieutenant Colonel after summer
manoeuvres. They gave him a battalion…

VASSA   I hear he drinks.

ANNA   Not enough. I put vodka in his tea sometimes but
it doesn't work – I dream about being a widow.
Can you imagine…?

VASSA   (*Smiling, quietly.*) Love has passed has it?

ANNA *is quiet, but smiles. She lights a cigarette.*

And it used to bubble. I remember I always told you...

ANNA   No. *Don't.* Stop.

VASSA   (*Examining her.*) Oh! Anna! You've changed. You used to be so timid, never even finished a sentence but now... such conviction! You sit there boldly, one leg over the other, telling your little old mother what to do. Smoking too.

ANNA   I know. I really love smoking.

PAVEL *is in the dining room. He quietly approaches the door, hears voices and presses his ear to the door.*

VASSA.   It doesn't suit a lady.

ANNA   It suits me.

VASSA   You dress like a lady.

ANNA   I dress how I like.

Beat.

VASSA   How are my grandsons?

ANNA   (*Proudly.*) Healthy, happy...

VASSA   Except the first one.

ANNA   The... sorry?

VASSA   Well he died didn't he?

ANNA   Oh I thought you meant the *living* grandchildren – yes Mum, the first one died... He was ill...

VASSA   Right so the first one was sick and died, but then after that came very happy and healthy ones. ... Interesting. Because presumably they came from exactly the same drinking, sick husband... I assume.

I mean they must've done, right?

ANNA *looks at her mother and laughs quietly.*

ANNA   So clever.

VASSA   Don't forget it.

            Beat.

            Now, we should call your brothers…

ANNA   Did they know I was coming?

            VASSA *goes to the door.*

VASSA   No. How would they? I didn't even know –

            She opens the door, PAVEL *is there, in a listening
            position. Caught out.*

            He stands.

PAVEL   I couldn't hear anything anyway.

VASSA   Really? What a shame. After all that.

PAVEL   (*Spitefully.*) Am I your child or not?

VASSA   (*Weary.*) What?

PAVEL   Because if I am, I have a right to know what's
            going on! They said a lady arrived with
            suitcases…

VASSA   Then just knock on the door, like a person, I'd
            open it and let you in. Quite simple…

ANNA   (*Coming forward.*) Hello Pavel!

PAVEL   (*To his mother.*) Ah! I had no idea! Anna!

VASSA   Over to you Anna. Ask him why he spies on his
            mother.

            She goes into the dining room.

PAVEL   It's a madhouse.

ANNA   (*Quietly, glancing into the dining room.*) She's
            still the same?

PAVEL	Worse. Since Dad got ill, she wants control over everything

PAVEL   Worse. Since Dad got ill, she wants control over everything·

ANNA   Surely she has that already...

PAVEL   Yes but she won't when Dad dies. We are not children any more, I'm twenty-four. Semyon's twenty-seven.

ANNA   Do you get on?

PAVEL   With Semyon. Sometimes. He's a bit idiotic but –

ANNA   And your wives?

PAVEL   His wife is cunning... and fat! Really massive. Anyway I don't care about them – look at you, you've become so beautiful! And so well dressed! Everyone here walks around like they're at a funeral.

ANNA   And you married Lyudmila.

PAVEL   Yes. But she's – it's dull because we aren't allowed to actually do anything. I started buying ancient icons from Old Believers, over the river, and Mother started getting at me: you don't believe in God she said, but you spend all this money! She doesn't understand that you can get ten roubles for every one that you spend... Selling antiques is a good business... one dealer in town bought six plates for nine roubles, then sold them for three hundred and twenty... But here it's just bricks, tiles, firewood, peat. It's not –

He sees PROKHOR *arriving.*

Oh... Here comes the antichrist.

PROKHOR   (*Enters.*) What a beautiful woman!

He holds out his arms, looks over his niece.

Give me a kiss...

ANNA   No.

PROKHOR   No?! Why not?

ANNA   Because I'm pretty sure it would be incredibly unpleasant. Ah, here's Semyon!

SEMYON *enters.*

You weren't lying Pavel, he's enormous!

PAVEL   Wait till you see his wife.

SEMYON   (*Happy.*) Anna! Wonderful! I'm so happy, look at you!

NATALYA *enters.*

PAVEL   See what I mean?

NATALYA   What?

ANNA   Introduce me to your wife Semyon.

SEMYON   Ah of course! Natalya, here's Anna! You remember I told you she always used to beat me?

PROKHOR   Not enough!

ANNA   (*To* NATALYA.) I'm so pleased to meet you. We shall be friends I think.

NATALYA   I'd like that.

SEMYON   My wife is very quiet. She is an Old Believer, christened at home in a big pot.

PROKHOR   Must've been huge!

ANNA   (*To* PAVEL.) And where's Lyudmila?

SEMYON *snorts with laughter, everyone is quiet for a second.*

PAVEL   Asleep I think.

SEMYON   You remember her?

ANNA   Yes, she was beautiful…

PROKHOR   Ah well, you should see her now. Time has not been kind.

ANNA   Really?

PROKHOR   Monstrous.

PAVEL   He's doing it to annoy me.

            NATALYA*'s been distracted.*

NATALYA   Wait –

PAVEL   They laugh at me. All the time.

NATALYA   What do you mean a *big pot*?!

PAVEL   They'll kill me Anna.

ANNA   Oh Pavel come on, ignore them –

            She puts her arm round PAVEL*'s shoulders and leads him into the corner, saying something to him; he mutters and waves his hands about.*

PROKHOR   (*To* SEMYON.) She's a beauty isn't she, your sister?

SEMYON   Ye-es…

NATALYA   Her eyes are too bright… like a cat.

SEMYON   Like Mum.

PROKHOR   And what a figure!

SEMYON   She was always a rebel. Back in the day. Did I say she used to beat me…

NATALYA   Yes you did. But it's bad of Lyudmila not to come and see her. It's disrespectful.

            MIKHAIL *enters.*

MIKHAIL   Anna Zakharovna! Let me congratulate you on your return to your own blood. To your own home.

NATALYA   *Her* home?! Don't think so –

MIKHAIL   I am immensely happy to see you…

ANNA   You don't look any older Misha! So good to see *you*.

SEMYON   (*To* NATALYA.) Do you like her?

NATALYA   She's gaudy.

SEMYON   Gaudy? She's wearing entirely one colour!

NATALYA   I meant her manner.

            LYUDMILA *enters. She's sleepy, dishevelled. She rushes to* ANNA.

LYUDMILA   Anna!

            ANNA *embraces her.*

ANNA   (*Embracing her.*) Lyuda!

LYUDMILA   Oh how wonderful...

ANNA   How beautiful you are!

LYUDMILA   Not like you. A ray of sunshine for us all here, stuck in the dark –

PAVEL   Here we go – the whining begins –

            VASSA *is suddenly at the doorway.*

VASSA   Anna go and see your father...

PROKHOR   (*Hopeful.*) What, why? Is he bad?

PAVEL   You can at least pretend you want him alive –

PROKHOR   If I was talking to you you'd know because I'd talk... really... slowly... and really... fucking... simply... because... you're... so... fucking... stuuuupid.

            PAVEL *slowly walks towards* PROKHOR. *Stands opposite him.*

            Then slaps him hard. LYUDMILA *screams then laughs.*

LYUDMILA   (*Laughing through tears.*) Ha! Look at him!

PROKHOR   (*Going after* PAVEL.) I'll rip your ears off!

PAVEL   You dare touch me…

MIKHAIL   (*To his daughter.*) Leave…

SEMYON   (*Excitedly.*) Uncle – stop him with a chair! Pavel, get under the table, come on! Ha ha! Ha ha!

As this carries on, VASSA *moves downstage, away from the chaos…*

She starts to scream.

Until…

End of Act One.

Curtain.

ACT TWO

Evening.

Twilight in the dining room. LYUDMILA *is in front of the stove.*

ANNA is smoking a cigarette and pacing the room, deep in thought.

ANNA   I was sorry you didn't write.

LYUDMILA   I didn't have your address.

ANNA   You could've found it.

LYUDMILA   Maybe but they watch me.

ANNA   Who?

LYUDMILA   Pavel. Dad. Everything I do. And anyway, what would I write? There's nothing interesting about me.

ANNA   Not true. Write anything! Your life. What's happened…

LYUDMILA   No. You wouldn't want a letter from me. The last two years, as each month's gone by, I've got more stupid. More bitter. I pretty much hate everyone.

ANNA   You shouldn't have married Pavel.

LYUDMILA   I had to.

ANNA   Oh.

            I see. How did that happen? You're so careful…

LYUDMILA   It was a strange time. Riots everywhere. The strikes, you know. It was like getting ready for a party. You're cleaning and tidying and putting everything in the right place in anticipation of this... revolution – but then it never happens. The party's suddenly cancelled. Anyway in the middle of all that he appeared... this really hot... almost a boy... but when he took his top off he was... I mean...

ANNA   Yes.

LYUDMILA   – and he was pockmarked.

ANNA   Pockmarked?

LYUDMILA   His face you know, because he was young, but Anna, he was *beautiful*.

ANNA   And what happened to him? Where is he now?

LYUDMILA   He disappeared.

ANNA   Does Pavel know?

LYUDMILA   No. No one knows apart from Prokhor.

ANNA   Prokhor? Why / would he –

LYUDMILA   He helped me get rid of it.

ANNA   I see.

LYUDMILA   Yeah, he was good, the pockmarked boy. Surprisingly gentle. And kind...

ANNA   I'm sure. But what about Prokhor?

LYUDMILA   Well you know, he's a businessman. He's fun... He's gentle too I suppose. He looks after you, but then...

ANNA   You have to give him something back.

LYUDMILA   With interest.

            Changes her tone.

            I don't want to say bad things about him, he was good to me. And we're not beggars, are we? We're civilised members of society, it wouldn't be right to get anything for free. We have to remember the good things people do for us. Isn't that right? And at some point, pay it back.

ANNA   (*Indifferently.*) I don't know.

LYUDMILA *smiles.*

LYUDMILA   I'm only really close to your mum. We hardly speak to each other and yes, she tells me off about Pavel all the time, I mean probably not as much as she should given it's her son but, I just *know* in my heart that she feels sorry for me and loves me. The only one who does. I mean if it wasn't for her – agh, what would I do?

ANNA   Yes? What would / you do?

LYUDMILA   – and when I'm sad there's the garden. I get so anxious in winter… but then I think 'here comes the spring!' And your mum and me begin to work. It's so wonderful to plant flowers! The sun comes up, and your mum knocks on my door: '*Stupid bitch*' she says, '*Get up.*' And together we go and garden, not talking to each other for almost the whole day! Oh it's perfect! You wouldn't recognise the garden! It's grown so much. Last spring we bought flower seeds, more than a hundred roubles' worth! I go to the peasants in the village and learn how to graft. Your mother bought me a little book about it – '*learn*' she said, '*you're a lazy cow and proper work will do you good!*' She always calls me a silly cow, or a stupid bitch, but she doesn't mean it really, it's just her little names, and yes, the peasants saw how well we did and they sent their wives for seeds, for grafts, and before I knew it, can you believe it?! – the peasants actually respected me! Because of the garden, life is wonderful in the spring, the summer, even the autumn… as I say it's only the winter that's hard.

Claustrophobic, stuck in the house. Of course we
don't say anything to each other then either, but
that's actually better because we know what we
are thinking and that's... Are you tired or
something?

ANNA   Why?

LYUDMILA   You don't look like you're listening.

ANNA   What? No it's just... I was amazed by how
            beautiful you are. So young!

LYUDMILA   You wait till the spring! You should see me then!
            Ah, our garden! I love the garden, I could / talk
            about it forever –

ANNA   (*Quickly.*) Hmm yes, Lyuda, let me / ask you
            about something –

LYUDMILA   – in the morning when it's sprinkled with dew
            and glistens in the sun

ANNA   Right –

LYUDMILA   – it's like walking into church, your head spins,
            your heart stops, I start to sing – it's like being
            drunk! Then if I stop singing for a moment, your
            mum cries – 'keep singing, bitch' and I see her
            face above the bushes – her gentle, kind,
            motherly face!

ANNA   (*Quietly, as if she doesn't believe her.*) Kind?

            A moment.

LYUDMILA   Remember how you and I played together in that
            garden?

ANNA   (*Soft.*) I do.

LYUDMILA   It's all I've got.

            PAVEL *enters and starts to light the candles in*
            the chandelier.

PAVEL   (*Enters*.) What are you girls giggling about?

ANNA   No one was giggling Pavel.

LYUDMILA Why are you doing that?

PAVEL   Because I want to see you, darling, I want to
             admire your beautiful / face –

LYUDMILA Put them out.

PAVEL   No.

LYUDMILA Freak.

             He winces. Tries to contain his anger.

PAVEL   Anna you see what a bitch I'm stuck with.

LYUDMILA Oh shut up. You crawled in front of me on your
             hands and knees like a beggar, '*please* Lyudmila,
             I'm *yours*! I'll do *anything*!'

ANNA.   Look come on –

LYUDMILA But he *can't* do anything, is the problem, not with
             me anyway, if you know what I mean, so he
             makes up for it by insulting me. It's what weak
             men do – call women names. I was given a pet,
             a Siberian cat –

PAVEL   Oh this again!

LYUDMILA He was called Gayev.

PAVEL   It scratched me.

LYUDMILA He poisoned it.

PAVEL   I didn't.

LYUDMILA It *died*.

PAVEL   Yes it *died* but I didn't poison it.

LYUDMILA What then?

PAVEL   It… ate itself…

LYUDMILA   It 'ate itself'?! Ha! Okay...

PAVEL   *Yes*, I saw it! Gayev was chewing his own leg off, probably couldn't stand to be near you.

LYUDMILA   You lie / all the time –

PAVEL   Sometimes when we're in conversation I have the same impulse, I think I'd rather start chewing / my own limbs –

LYUDMILA   Shut up shut up shut up shut up shut up shut up I can't hear you any more I don't want to see you I don't want any of you.

She leaves quickly.

ANNA *sits. Looking at* PAVEL. *He covers.*

PAVEL   Yeah... Always runs away when she's losing. She can't bear to look at me cos she knows what she's done. She knows how... evil she is.

ANNA   What are you going to do Pavel?

PAVEL   What do you mean?

ANNA   She's your wife.

He smiles.

PAVEL   Do? Nothing. She makes my life hell. She might as well suffer too...

Suddenly, passionately and sincerely.

Oh but Jesus Annie you're right! Help me! I'll give you whatever you want. Money, if you need it. I'll give you so much money when Dad dies!

ANNA   What can I do?

PAVEL   You can teach her to love me. Cos honestly, it might not look like it, but I adore her.

ANNA   You – Yes you're right it doesn't really / look like that –

PAVEL   There's no end to my love! When she sleeps
               I kneel by the bed: 'Lyuda, Lyudochka, no one
               loves you like I do!' I whisper to her like that all
               night. It's the best time because she doesn't hear
               it? And can't answer back.

ANNA   Yeah I'm not really sure that's okay?

PAVEL   I tell her, when she's sleeping 'Everyone else has
               something to distract them, but I'm a freak so
               I don't have anything to live for except for you.'
               I say it most nights. In her ear.

ANNA   It's quite creepy Pavel.

PAVEL   No, it's *romantic*! Anyway you've got to help me!

ANNA   Alright, calm down, someone's coming…

PAVEL   I don't care! Let them come! Let them all come.

               NATALYA *enters*.

               They should all know!

NATALYA   Know what?

PAVEL   Nothing.

NATALYA   Your mother is calling for you…

               NATALYA *looks at them suspiciously*.

               And she's angry.

               PAVEL *starts to go*.

PAVEL   She's always angry.

NATALYA   Apparently you beat the office boy.

PAVEL   So? You have to beat them or they don't respect
               you.

               He goes. NATALYA *makes to go too*.

ANNA   (*To* NATALYA.) Natalya, have you got a moment?

NATALYA   (*Coming back*.) What?

ANNA   No just...

            She breathes out.

            He's worn me out!

NATALYA   I know that feeling. Was he complaining about
            his wife?

ANNA   You seem to get on with him. Almost the only
            one who does.

NATALYA   Yes, well I make it a rule to get on equally with
            everyone.

ANNA   Sounds a bit boring. The least you could do is
            take an odd dislike to someone. Everyone else
            seems to.

NATALYA   My husband is entertainment enough.

ANNA   Really?

NATALYA   Yes. He works hard to you know... make me
            laugh. And all that.

            Anyway it's not really the time for laughter is it?

ANNA   (*Becoming interested.*) Why not?

NATALYA   (*With conviction.*) Well no one can live now like
            before. Out here. People should move into town.
            Everything has to change.

            Beat.

ANNA   Go on.

NATALYA   No just, I think about it a lot... I... I think we
            should live in gated, fenced-off communities,
            where there are lots of police outside. And troops.
            Because the last few years have been terrible,
            haven't they? Quiet people, just like what you
            thought were normal people, they're beginning to
            change. Everyone's started to *think* and secretly
            talk to one another and strange people are
            everywhere. One was here, trying to persuade

anyone who'd listen that all business is a sin!
I mean I was really scared... just think what will
happen if people aren't working?

ANNA   You're quite a thinker.

NATALYA   Yes well I have a sick child so I don't sleep much
at night. I'm always thinking. About lots of
things. But no one listens to me...

Except now! Here you are listening. It makes
a nice change!

I know they say things about me.

I've also been thinking about the –

PROKHOR *enters, suddenly. He's angry.*

PROKHOR   Where's Vassa?

ANNA   No idea.

NATALYA   She went to the factory.

PROKHOR   Did she? Stupid cow.

ANNA   Look at you! Where on earth have you been?

PROKHOR   The dovecot. I've been asking those slaves we
employ to fix the ladder for three months, *three
months*, but they don't! They're doing it on
purpose Anna, I'm telling you. If I fall into the
cellar and break my neck, it will be entirely
deliberate. Pavel's doing, probably...

ANNA   Come on, he doesn't want to kill you –

PROKHOR   You have no idea – last time I was sitting in the
dovecot, someone quietly opened the hatch to the
cellar, moved the ladder to the edge and then
suddenly, the door to the courtyard slammed shut.
It was dark and the floor was wet. I barely
managed to get out alive. So what am I supposed
to think? Someone did it. And who's most likely?
Who's got the unique combination of motive and
utter incompetence?

NATALYA   (*To* ANNA.) It's true Anna, if Pavel is provoked
he could do something terrible. He's the type.
You know, because he's... because of his...
I warned Lyudmila...

PROKHOR   You see? Even the donkey says the same thing...

NATALYA   The – There's no / need to call me a donkey.

ANNA   Natalya, don't make him more paranoid than he
already is –

NATALYA   Just because he's paranoid doesn't mean it isn't
true. Unhappy people can be terribly mean...

PROKHOR   (*Joyfully.*) Ah! Look at that. This little pigeon has
a mind like a snake. Love it.

NATALYA *stands, to go –*

NATALYA   Excuse me.

She turns back.

I'm not a pigeon. Or a snake. Or a donkey. I'm
just a normal... human being.

She goes.

PROKHOR   A dark soul, in a dark dress.

He laughs.

You know I heard her once with her husband,
dreaming about the future.

Imitates her.

'Semyon, Semyon! I'll be there, lying in a velvet
dressing gown, and under that, all there is, is
a lace shirt, or maybe nothing at all, and I'm
sitting on a beautiful quelque-chose'...

ANNA   (*Smiling.*) Don't you mean chaise-longue?

PROKHOR   I know what I mean! 'And all these people come
and visit us; oh hello police-chief! Hi there
judges and oh! The mayor! What an honour! The

whole town is here! And they're all just...
looking at me, so envious of *you* – oh, yes,
Zheleznov! What a wife he's got! And I move my
little foot like this, and then I show them my
shoulder – let them drool!'

He laughs.

Come on! It's a good impression. Semyon's such
a dick, I do it for him, and he just laughs. He
laughs when he doesn't know what's going on,
which is pretty much all the time.

ANNA   (*Seriously.*) She's a strange woman. Like she's
                naive but –

PROKHOR   Yes, God knows what she really thinks. She rolls
                her eyes at me constantly. They all do. Agh,
                I have had enough of them all!...

ANNA   Then why stay?

PROKHOR   Why do you think?! My money's tied up here,
                praise be to Zakhar. Once I'm allowed to take it,
                it'll be goodbye family of thieves...

ANNA   And where then?

PROKHOR   Moscow, of course!

He leans towards her, secretly.

For in Moscow, Anna, I have the ripening fruit of
an unhappy affair.

ANNA   Really? Tell me.

PROKHOR   He's a student. With a superb face and an
                excellent future –

ANNA   Who's the mother?

PROKHOR   Oh. Ah. She died. Unfortunately.

Lively once again.

He calls me his unexpected dad. And clearly he's
not related to us because he doesn't *ask* for

anything. Can you imagine that? No demands at
all. He just drinks, goes to the theatre, knows all
the actresses… And studies myths at university.

ANNA   Maths?

PROKHOR   *Myths*. The science of mythology. He told me
about it in detail. Odysseus! What a bastard! And
an excellent liar! Pretended he went down to hell,
and he said that in hell, nothing was scary, just
really boring, which I get. Pyotr, my boy, he's
a good liar too. One of the best I've known. So
proud. I'm considering making him –

VASSA enters.

VASSA   (*Enters.*) Why is Natalya so angry? Who did it?
She's standing in the middle of my dining room
ripping the tassles off her shawl. There's tassles
everywhere.

She turns to PROKHOR.

Prokhor, your pigeon man is asking for you.

PROKHOR   Eurgh. He can wait…

ANNA *uses her eyes and hand movements to
gesture for her mother to leave.* VASSA *looks at
her incredulously.*

ANNA   Is Semyon back from town?

VASSA   I don't know. No one's told me, and I haven't…

ANNA *gestures.*

…seen him…

More gestures from ANNA.

But I… suppose I'll… go and look…

VASSA *leaves.*

PROKHOR   Let's play cards. Call Lyudmila and Natalya…

ANNA   Oh, alright. Good idea – So you'll be leaving the
            business?

PROKHOR   Yes, too old for all that. And what is it anyway?
            It frightens me these days. You used to walk in
            the village and feel like the lord of the manor.
            Now people still bow, but they do it sarcastically.
            To hide their spiteful eyes. It's like the *Iliad*. You
            know the *Iliad*?

ANNA   Of course.

PROKHOR   All of them trying to bash each other on the head.
            Every man for himself! Can't last. I wasn't ever
            much of a businessman. What would I need it for?

            SEMYON *enters, importantly.*

SEMYON   Who wanted me?

ANNA   Mum.

SEMYON   She just said you did.

            So nobody wants me?

            Oh.

PROKHOR   Another excellent interjection Semyon.

            He shouts –

            Lyudmila!

            He gets up to go. Turns to SEMYON.

            You want to play cards?

SEMYON   Could do.

            (*To* ANNA.) Ah, Anna! From the town.

ANNA   That's right.

SEMYON   Town's brilliant isn't it?

ANNA   I like it yes.

SEMYON   Everything is so… solid. Bright, and clean. The
            conversation is so much *broader*, don't you
            think? Because people in town *know* about
            everything. And the Duma's there, all different
            types of view, of politics. Real diversity. I *love*
            diversity. Interesting things happening every
            minute… It's so much more beautiful. The
            buildings, the art –

PROKHOR   (*As he goes*.)… the women.

            SEMYON *calls after* PROKHOR.

SEMYON   I – *no* actually!

            (*To* ANNA.) I'm sorry you had to hear that. You
            can tell *he's* not from the town. Talking about
            women in that way.

ANNA   You really think he's messing around with
            Lyudmila?

SEMYON   You make it sound like they're teenagers.

ANNA   Well she practically is.

SEMYON   Aha! Yes I suppose so. You choose your words
            carefully. Course you do, being from the town.
            Yes Prokhor's definitely 'messing around'…
            I heard him giving her a lesson one day. My eyes
            practically popped out of my head.

ANNA   What was he teaching her?

            SEMYON *laughs, embarrassed. But* ANNA's
            straight – serious.

            Well?

SEMYON   I can't tell you.

ANNA   I'm married.

SEMYON   All the same.

ANNA   Seen more of this world than you, Semyon,
            I promise.

SEMYON   Right... Well. I'm sure that's...

           To be completely honest I didn't understand what
           it meant...

           Something about children. How to make sure
           children aren't born...?

           He laughs, unsure of himself.

           Anyway, he's an idiot. Doesn't understand the
           business like the rest of us.

ANNA   You like the business then?

SEMYON   Me? Yes, but there isn't much joy in tiles and
           bricks, and everyone's so depressed now. Police.
           Strict rules. Alcoholics and fighting. When Dad
           dies I'll live in town, like you. With all the good,
           clever people. Everyone in the country is so
           ignorant. Fucking awful, frankly.

ANNA   But what about the business?

SEMYON   Ah, cut it back. It's got no future, working with
           peat. And what's left of it, Mum and Mikhail can
           sort it out. Whilst I will open a jewellery shop in
           town! On the main street, on Dvoryanskaya. It'll
           have a name, and a sign.

ANNA   What's the name?

SEMYON   Hmm I'm very proud of the name. Natalya and
           I spent hours on it.

ANNA   What is it?

SEMYON   Ready?

ANNA   Yes.

SEMYON   'Semyon Zheleznov's Jewellery Shop.'

ANNA   Lovely.

SEMYON   I've drawn a little picture, how it'll look. I'll
           show you –

He gets a small drawing from his pocket –

ANNA   No it's alright you don't need to –

SEMYON   Here.

            She looks, turns the picture the other way up.

ANNA   Right. Yes. That's… a shop.

SEMYON   Ah! Jewellery! It's such a soft word! Isn't it?

ANNA   Well, I –

SEMYON   '*Jewellery.*'

ANNA   Yes it's a… good word.

SEMYON   J!

ANNA   Bless you.

SEMYON   No. 'J'! The 'J' in jewellery. The sheer sound of
            it! I'll have an apartment above the shop. And
            buy a harmonica. And play it.

            J!

            He laughs.

            J!

            LYUDMILA *comes running in.*

ANNA   (*To herself.*) Oh thank god.

            (*To* LYUDMILA.) What?

LYUDMILA   Anna, stop them!

            SEMYON *jumps up, scared.*

SEMYON   Stop who?

LYUDMILA   Uncle Prokhor is beating up Pavel…

SEMYON   See what I mean? Country people. That's the
            complete opposite of 'J' isn't it? Well? What are
            you waiting for Anna? Go on!

ANNA   Why should I go? You go!

SEMYON   Me?!

           ANNA *and* LYUDMILA *just look at him.*

           Oh. Right then.

           As he goes.

           I'm not a fucking policeman…

           A moment.

LYUDMILA   I wish Prokhor would just kill Pavel. Put him out
           of his misery.

ANNA   Why are they fighting?

LYUDMILA   Pavel said he wouldn't let me play cards. I thought
           it was funny so I laughed at him, then he pushed
           me, so Prokhor got him by the hair…

ANNA   I don't know how you can live like this Lyuda.

LYUDMILA   Happiness costs a lot.

           She's pensive.

           But you have to keep trying. If you can ever get
           a few seconds of it, you remember it forever, and
           it makes things easier.

           Anna, don't you think it's wonderful when a man
           cries in front of you?

ANNA   Yes I normally enjoy it.

LYUDMILA   From joy I mean –

ANNA   Oh right.

LYUDMILA   He's so sweet in that moment! Pouring his heart
           out. Makes you feel like the richest queen. Don't
           you think? You have no regrets, you would take
           death even…

           VASSA *enters.*

VASSA   What's the noise?

LYUDMILA Oh Mum! Please! Help me –

VASSA Why? What have you done?

LYUDMILA Nothing! They're fighting – Pavel and Prokhor.

VASSA Again? I told you Lyuda...

LYUDMILA I tried but you understand. I can't be like that
with him. 'Loving and kind.' You said it yourself,
you can't lie to a man. Well, not when you see
him all the time.

VASSA Lyudmila, it's quite simple, they're both pricks.
And it's up to you to sort them out.

LYUDMILA How?!

VASSA *just stares at her.* LYUDMILA *rolls her
eyes, then goes.*

VASSA *sits by the stove.*

ANNA Does this sort of thing happen often?

VASSA Only for the last two or three years. Sometimes it
feels like my heart's being squeezed... If I could
I would take them all and...

I do pity Pavel.

ANNA It's not great for Lyudmila either.

VASSA It would be fine if she learnt to control herself.

ANNA What's she doing with Prokhor?

VASSA Prokhor discovers a girl's secret and uses it...

But there's no...

I can't do anything about him so...

ANNA (*Quietly.*) When you go to bed, I will come and
see you. We need to talk. They've all just
confessed to me.

VASSA Even Prokhor?

ANNA	Did you know he has a son?
VASSA	Not just the one, I bet.
ANNA	Well possibly, but this one he was talking about, he wants to adopt him.

VASSA stands.

VASSA	(*Getting up.*) He...?

You're trying to scare me.

ANNA	No. Just telling you / what he said.
VASSA	So there's the end! Of everything we've been working for. Everything we might be proud of. Zakhar dies, Prokhor gets his money, and the moment he adopts that boy it'll be his too. Another one in the way.

She thinks.

It can't happen. What else?

ANNA	Semyon wants to move to town...
VASSA	No surprise there. What about Pavel?
ANNA	He wants to move to town too.
VASSA	(*Gruffly.*) Him?! Oh come on. No that won't work. I'll find him somewhere to go.

PROKHOR, SEMYON *and* NATALYA *all enter, agitated.*

SEMYON	Natalya... Just... / Natalya stop!
PROKHOR	Get this stupid / woman off me!
NATALYA	Someone has to say it like it is.
SEMYON	Natalya! J!
NATALYA	What? No –
SEMYON	Why do you care about / them anyway?
VASSA	What's going on?

PROKHOR   Your daughter-in-law is having a / hissy fit.

NATALYA   You're the one who's turned / Pavel into
            a savage...

PROKHOR   Semyon, you twat / shut her up.

ANNA   Uncle, you're the cleverest person here...

PROKHOR   Yes, I should be, but they turn me / completely
            insane.

ANNA   So just calm down –

PROKHOR   He's a fucking terrorist! Waving a knife at me –

NATALYA   It's all your fault! It's what you did!

            Enter LYUDMILA. *She sits in the corner and
            watches everyone without moving.*

VASSA   Semyon! Control your wife!

SEMYON   Mum don't *speak to me like that*! I'm not *three*.

VASSA   Then stop acting / like a toddler –

SEMYON   And you always say *control*! You just fucking /
            love control, don't you?

NATALYA   You ruined Lyudmila...

SEMYON   But / soon –

PROKHOR   Not me you / stupid bitch –

SEMYON   Soon there'll be no one left / to boss around and
            then –

PROKHOR   – she ruined herself before she got married. Anna,
            I don't know what she's told you, but you do
            realise Lyudmila's not as pure as you think, way
            before all this she had a bit of trouble and needed
            a –

            He notices LYUDMILA.

            Oh.

LYUDMILA   Yes I'm here, go on. Tell them then! Tell them what happened.

VASSA   (*Sternly, quietly.*) Lyudka!

PROKHOR   Oh… just fuck off / all of you.

LYUDMILA   No come on! Don't stop now! You've set it up, *uncle*.

Beat.

Knock it down.

PROKHOR   I'll cut your tongue out.

LYUDMILA   *Tell them!*

A moment.

Then PROKHOR *storms out.*

Aah. Chickened out… I wonder why!

VASSA   Stop talking. Now.

LYUDMILA   But Mum it doesn't matter! Pavel's going to find out. Everyone's going to find out!

SEMYON   (*To his wife.*) We should leave –

LYUDMILA   – cos Natalya's heard everything, and she's not physically capable of keeping things to herself.

NATALYA   Er I might not be perfect but I'm unfailingly loyal, I'm certainly –

SEMYON   Natka! Remember – J!

That's all that matters! Come on! Let's go.

J!

NATALYA *looks at him. Then sighs and goes.*

NATALYA   If it stops you making that stupid fucking noise –

SEMYON *quickly follows her.*

VASSA   You see Anna? They just grab what they can, and leave –

LYUDMILA I don't. Nothing to grab. I don't want anything! Just my life, my *life*...

PAVEL *enters with a bandaged forehead.*

PAVEL Mum I demand my inheritance. Right now.

LYUDMILA (*Half-laughing, half-smiling.*) Ah, look at my husband! What a catch.

VASSA Here's another one, his tongue hanging out, desperate –

PAVEL Mum are you talking to me?

VASSA No Pavel I'm talking *about* you.

PAVEL Anna, tell her she needs to give me what's mine and let me go...

VASSA You'll be going somewhere soon enough.

PAVEL Really? Where? And why are you saying it like that?

ANNA Mum I actually think you should. If he's stuck here... Prokhor attacks him all the time... who knows what might happen?

VASSA What do you mean?

PAVEL I'm not afraid of him!

ANNA Look – Prokhor beat him up.

PAVEL It was a fight, actually, two-way. He didn't / beat me up –

ANNA Yes he's weak but even the weak get angry and lash out sometimes... and well... what might happen then?

VASSA *stares at her a second, then –*

VASSA Enough.

LYUDMILA No no carry on Anna what do you mean...?

VASSA   Lyudmila get out! Pavel, you too.

             *They both exit. VASSA walks about the room,
             stopping in front of her daughter.*

             What made you think that up?

ANNA   (*Innocently.*) Think what up?

VASSA   I see through you. You think if your brother
             torments your uncle... If he attacks him... and
             kills him, he'll go to jail and you'll get the lot.

ANNA   Mum! What are you talking about?

VASSA   (*Threateningly.*) You're not as clever as you
             think.

ANNA   I'm as clever as I need to be.

             A noise.

VASSA   Who's that?

             MIKHAIL *enters.*

             Oh. Well? Yes? What?

MIKHAIL   He's finding it hard to breathe.

VASSA   Ohhhh, I wish God would just take him. He's
             been gasping his last breath for five weeks now.
             What's awful is his eyes are bright. He
             understands everything.

MIKHAIL   He's not long left.

             Beat.

VASSA   Wait here...

             She goes.

ANNA   Life is hard Mikhail.

MIKHAIL   Yup. Couldn't be worse.

ANNA   But how does it end?

             He shrugs.

It's so difficult for Mum, and Prokhor clearly doesn't want to help...

MIKHAIL   (*Despondently.*) Huh! Him? Help? Not likely. Your father used to say that a Russian man often mistakes his stupidity for conscience... That's Prokhor.

LIPA *enters, and stops, a little unsure.*

Yes?

LIPA   Anna Zakharovna – Prokhor wants you to go and see him.

ANNA   Why?

LIPA   His heart isn't good.

ANNA   (*Questioningly, to* MIKHAIL.) What does that mean?

MIKHAIL   (*Reassuring her.*) It happens to him sometimes.

LIPA   He struggles to catch his breath.

MIKHAIL   (*Glancing at* LIPA.) Yes he gets breathless... Lipa here knows all about it...

ANNA   Alright.

ANNA *exits quickly.* MIKHAIL *stops* LIPA *with a gesture.*

MIKHAIL   Well?

LIPA   I won't.

MIKHAIL   Why not?

LIPA   It's not right.

MIKHAIL   Not / right?

LIPA   Whatever he's done, he's a human being.

MIKHAIL   'Not right'? Let's get this straight –

LIPA   – No please –

MIKHAIL	– It's fine to suffocate your own son –
LIPA	Don't –
MIKHAIL	– but it's 'not right' to do it to someone very old you're not related to. What's the difference? You're saying a child isn't a human being?
LIPA	(*Furiously.*) I did it out of pity…
MIKHAIL	(*Softer.*) Just listen you fucking witch! Prokhor *knows* what you did. So getting this done, right now, would help *you*, wouldn't it?
LIPA	You know. Should I poison you too?!
MIKHAIL	*Stop shouting.* Be careful, I can arrange accidents for anyone.

He bends down to her.

This is the perfect moment. You just give him a little more than normal from the two vials. And it's not poison. It's lovely, tasty, completely normal medicine. When you're finished you go wherever you want with God's blessing! Cos without sin, Lipa, there's no repentance. And without repentance there's no salvation. So you're fine! Go!

She doesn't.

You'll get such a reward for this. You're young, and you must *live*, but I'm telling you, if you don't sin occasionally you won't survive.

Or doesn't freedom matter to you?

LIPA	Of course.

It's all that matters –

LIPA *goes, yielding to his pressure.*

Fucking crocodile tears –

PAVEL *looks in.*

PAVEL	Where's Mum?
MIKHAIL	She went to see your father.
PAVEL	Who were you talking to?
MIKHAIL	Myself.
PAVEL	Then congratulations Mikhail! At last you've found yourself a friend! Watch out though, he'll cheat you!
MIKHAIL	Thank you for the warning Pavel. I'll take it as reward for everything I've done for you over the course of your life.
PAVEL	Yes. Well. I'll... I'll just... You take it as a reward and I'll...

He's got nothing.

He turns and goes. MIKHAIL *paces, hands behind his back, clicking his fingers.*

Enter VASSA, SEMYON *and* NATALYA.

VASSA	(*Gloomily to* MIKHAIL.) You're right. Zakhar's eyes are closed now. He's near the end.
MIKHAIL	(*Looking down.*) Prokhor's had another seizure...
VASSA	(*To her children.*) What are you all doing here?
SEMYON	What are *you* doing here?
VASSA	Go and get Father Yegor!...
	Well? Natalya? Go away.
NATALYA	No, I really have to protest that –
SEMYON	Natalya! J!

He goes.

VASSA	What on earth was that noise?
NATALYA	Oh it's just his...

She sighs. Tired of it all.

Doesn't matter.

VASSA   Go to your room.

NATALYA   My – No, please. Not my room. It's… frightening
           in there.

VASSA   Frightening?

NATALYA   I can hear him… wheezing…

VASSA   Oh don't be rididiculous. I know the sound of
           death's a bit… distracting, but all of us are
           doomed to die one day. I'm older than you, and
           I'm not frightened… Just try to ignore it. Sing,
           or something.

           NATALYA *exits quietly, wrapped in a shawl.*

           Afraid? She's not afraid of eating my bread.

           Prokhor had a seizure?

MIKHAIL   (*Quietly.*) Yes madam.

           A sudden noise.

           What was that?

ANNA   (*Runs in, frightenened, whispering.*) Lipa has
           poisoned Uncle!

VASSA   Poisoned? Is he dead?

ANNA   I don't know… No. Not yet –

MIKHAIL   (*Hurriedly.*) Right… not dead? Right.

           Well, the police… I suppose we have to call the
           police…

VASSA   Wait! Where are you going? *Wait.*

           He does.

           Anna, stop fussing…

ANNA   She's in there screaming… just standing completely still and screaming and / screaming.

VASSA   Bring her here…

ANNA   We need to call a doctor…

VASSA   (*Sternly, quietly.*) *No. Wait*, I said!

LIPA runs in, throws herself at ANNA.

What have you done?

LIPA   (*Throws herself on VASSA.*) Oh God, he made me! It was him, he did everything!

VASSA   It was the first time you've given him his medicine, yes?

LIPA   No.

VASSA   You didn't know how much to give him…

LIPA   No! Let me go, / for God's sake!

VASSA   You know that people go to prison for mistakes like that?

LIPA   (*Not understanding anything.*) What will happen? Oh, what will happen to me?

MIKHAIL   God she's useless. Excuse me I'll sort her out –

VASSA   In here.

VASSA pushes LIPA into her study.

Sssssssssssshhh! Sit down.

Sit down.

Down.

She finally does. Then VASSA turns to ANNA.

Right – Oh. Now what's wrong with *you*? Why are you trembling? A mistake happened, the girl didn't give him the right medicine… The master of the house is dying, there is chaos, a girl on her own, rushed off her feet…

ANNA   (*Quietly.*) Yes. I see.

VASSA   What? There's nothing to see! Go to your uncle
                and help…

NATALYA   (*Running in.*) Come quickly – Prokhor –

ANNA   (*Involuntarily.*) Is he dead?

NATALYA   (*Taken aback.*) Dead? *Dead?* Why would you
                suddenly / ask that –

VASSA   (*Glancing at* NATALYA.) Yes exactly Anna!
                Come on! Why would he *die* from a seizure?

                He has them all the time. He's had two this
                winter already!

NATALYA   Yes but actually it was horrific. He just crawled
                from his bed… twitching… hiccuping…

VASSA   Hiccuping! Oh well, you know I get hiccups after
                dinner sometimes and it's annoying, isn't it?
                Some people find it funny but I don't. Just go to
                him… both of you, go and help.

NATALYA   Yes. Come on.

                ANNA, *frightened, looks at her mother, and exits
                after* NATALYA. VASSA *walks into her study,
                goes up to* LIPA *who is paralysed, pushes her.*

VASSA   *Wake up*. He's alive, you hear? Alive!

LIPA   Oh thank God.

VASSA   You better disappear before you're torn apart.

MIKHAIL   (*To* LIPA.) You'll pay for this mistake.

VASSA   Leave her alone.

LIPA   (*Falling on her knees.*) Vassa Petrovna. I did it
                deliberately. He taught me how. Him. There! My
                own Vassa. Understand. Forgive me.

VASSA   Go to your room!

LIPA   (*Standing up.*) I'm innocent… God knows…
              He knows.

              She staggers out.

              VASSA *and* MIKHAIL *look at each other.*
              MIKHAIL *hangs his head guiltily.*

VASSA   You idiot.

MIKHAIL   She must have done it wrong…

VASSA   That chemist.

MIKHAIL   I'm telling you, she didn't do it right –

VASSA   And I'm an idiot for trusting you. Well? What
              now?

              Let's talk.

              She goes into her study.

              The first thing is Lipa: watch her! She mustn't
              speak to anyone!

              End of Act Two.

              Curtain.

              A caption appears:

              INTERVAL

ACT THREE

The dining room. The doors are closed. VASSA *is by the stove, dressed in mourning.* ANNA *is pacing and smoking.* SEMYON *sits at the table.*

SEMYON   (*Yawning.*) We should have some tea. It's time.

VASSA   It hasn't been forty minutes.

SEMYON   So what? Forty minutes? It's my life. I can delete forty minutes. I can delete a whole hour if I want. Or a month…

     He puts his feet on a chair. Then takes them down. Then puts them up again.

VASSA   What are you doing?

SEMYON   I'm bored! My wife's unwell. We can't play cards. My blood is congealing from having *nothing to do.*

VASSA   It hasn't been forty days since your father died and you're wanting to play cards…

SEMYON   Forty days, forty minutes. Please just let's be happy!

VASSA   And why does Natalya suffer from nerves anyway? I'm nearly sixty and they've never troubled me…

     ANNA *throws her cigarette butt in the stove.*

ANNA   My nerves are bad too. This house is huge and echoey, there's often this kind of rustling…

VASSA   Rats.

     Or Prokhor's pigeons.

Or the cat.

Or sometimes all of them, eating each other…

ANNA   Things creak at night.

VASSA   The wood is dry.

ANNA   The shadows move.

VASSA   Well that's Lipa. Walking around…

SEMYON   Mum! Don't bring her up.

VASSA   (*Pondering.*) I've heard her –

ANNA   You don't believe in ghosts!

VASSA   She took her own life. It's quite possible. How it works.

SEMYON   This same old song – Mum you don't believe in anything but cash.

VASSA   (*Harmlessly.*) You are a moron Semyon! Why do you think your dad and I saved our money? For our *children*. But it turns out they're not worth those roubles. You couldn't even give me a healthy grandson…

SEMYON   (*Gruffly.*) It's not true –

VASSA   What's not true?

ANNA   Semyon –

SEMYON   I gave you a grandson.

VASSA   From the maid.

SEMYON   Yes but that still counts! You put us together, from what I recall –

VASSA   Anyway the child was stillborn so –

SEMYON   (*Starts.*) He wasn't stillborn, she did it herself! She told Natalya everything, so you can stop lying. You made her life hell till she did it and once it was done, you threatened her with that child her whole life. That's why she hung herself…

VASSA   (*Calmly.*) Well, Anna, listen to that…

ANNA   (*Indignantly.*) How can you say such filth Semyon? It's horrible…

SEMYON   There is no point sucking up to our mother Anna… don't know what she's promised you but she won't pay your bills. No way.

He exits, banging the door hard.

VASSA   (*Smirking/chuckling.*) Well!

ANNA   Agh, Mum! I'm getting now how hard it's been.

VASSA   It's fine. And it's important you understand what's happening –

ANNA   Sometimes I'm scared for you…

VASSA   There are so many different thoughts swarming in my little head. They buzz like wasps, but there's no answer to them, no solution!…

Pause.

Have you thought why men seem to take after their fathers, not their mothers? You'll start to think that too, just wait and see… There I was, stupidly trying to protect Semyon's… health by letting him have a lover in the house, so at least we'd know who she was, and he goes and gets her pregnant. Then it turned out to be pointless as he subsequently went and caught something in the village anyway –

ANNA   (*Quietly.*) Is it really true that the baby…

VASSA   No. A bit. So what if it is? What was I supposed to do?

ANNA   So Lyudmila got pregnant and got rid of it, and to cover it up you made her marry your son, but then she was blackmailed into sex with your brother-in-law. Meanwhile Semyon did it with the maid who gave birth to a baby which for some reason she killed, then you forced her to attempt to poison your brother but after she failed you tormented her until she killed herself. And at some point in all this, Semyon had sex with someone *else* in the village and got venereal disease.

VASSA *looks at* ANNA.

VASSA	Don't judge me Anna. You've got children and when it comes to it you'll do the same. Whatever it takes to protect your flesh and blood.
ANNA	I doubt I'd go that far.
VASSA	One day you'll have to. Maybe soon.

Beat. ANNA *a little unnerved.*

ANNA	So anyway, Prokhor has written two letters to his son...
VASSA	About what?
ANNA	He wants him to come here.
VASSA	To us. Why?
ANNA	(*Takes out the letters.*) I assume the adoption. Here...
VASSA	You have them?... Aha! Good.
ANNA	I thought perhaps they shouldn't be sent.
VASSA	You're right! Clever girl. Turns out you are a woman in this family after all! You see? It's not dogs that guard a house, it's us!

She goes to her daughter, puts her hands on her shoulders.

Sell them to me.

ANNA	What?

VASSA   A hundred for both. What do you think? I know you need the money.

ANNA   I… No, just… take them… that's… I'm your daughter, we're doing this together. Why would you say that?

VASSA   Don't be offended. As you say I'm a mother. And as we've established I'll do what it takes.

ANNA   But even so…

VASSA   (*Hiding the letters.*) Mothers are all sinners. God's judgement on us will be terrible no doubt, but I won't repent before people! When the time comes I'll explain it all to the Virgin Mother and she'll understand! She pities evil mothers like you and me.

ANNA   But what about the letters? When he gets better won't he write more and send them himself? And he asked me to send them registered – he'll want to see the proofs of postage?

VASSA   Oh that's easy. There's old ones in the office. Mikhail will sort it – he copies the surname and address, stamps them… not a problem. When your father was carrying on with some blonde in town we used to do it! Just make sure Prokhor doesn't send them via anyone else.

ANNA   Right…

VASSA   – like Lyudmila. She's a child. He'll persuade her –

ANNA   They're arguing at the moment, and anyway she tells me everything.

VASSA   Remember if Prokhor leaves his money with us, your children benefit too.

ANNA   Mum! That's got nothing to do with why I'm –

VASSA   Bull shit. Don't pretend. Everyone's out for themselves. They always are. I wear glasses, I see everything... And that's how you must be with me. No lies. Straight dealing. The receipt, yes? That's what you want.

ANNA The receipt, yes.

VASSA Good then.

Beat.

ANNA It's like I'm seeing the real you for the first time today.

VASSA Yes it takes a long time to really *see* one's mother. And you may not like what you find.

Someone's coming...

The door opens quietly – NATALYA, *pale and wan, enters.*

NATALYA I was informed it was time for tea... but it's not ready...

VASSA Well lay the table then... Where's Lyudmila?

NATALYA Prokhor called for her.

VASSA Ah. Right –

She makes eyes at ANNA, *wanting her to leave.* ANNA *doesn't understand.*

Anna, maybe go and ask Prokhor if he might drink tea with us?

ANNA Yes.

She goes.

VASSA Do you feel better?

NATALYA I can't sleep, and my heart aches... Klyamzinskii the clerk's wife came to see me again...

VASSA She shouldn't have bothered.

NATALYA She was crying.

VASSA	She shouldn't have bothered with that either. Tears won't clean a footcloth.

DUNYA enters, bowing silently. NATALYA stops laying out the dishes, lets DUNYA take over. VASSA paces around the room, pushing her glasses up on her forehead.

NATALYA	You should forgive him… in memory of the dead.
VASSA	The dead are… well… dead. And you shouldn't interfere in my business…
NATALYA	But I feel sorry for these people!

DUNYA goes out.

VASSA	If they don't want to work that's their problem. And you'd do the same – when you had a lazy nanny – didn't you get rid of her?
NATALYA	Yes but it was a baby…
VASSA	Well I have children too and they need good workers. If, when I die, I leave them drunks and idlers, what kind of mother does that make me?

DUNYA comes back in, carrying the samovar.

Dunya! You're splashing it on the floor!

DUNYA	I'm sorry Vassa.

She puts it down, and is about to go when –

VASSA	And Dunya, you may go and see the priest, as we spoke about.
DUNYA	The priest. Yes.

VASSA gives her a piece of paper.

VASSA	Say you are there with my blessing.

DUNYA looks at her.

DUNYA	Yes. Of course, Vassa Zhlezenova.

DUNYA *goes.*

VASSA She's a good girl, that one. Despite everything.

PAVEL *enters; he is a little drunk, sits at the table.*

Oh Pavel! Look what a mess you've made!

PAVEL Have I? Oh. So what?

ANNA (*Shouts in the doorway.*) Mum!

VASSA What?

She goes. A moment.

NATALYA Lyudmila has reconciled with Prokhor.

PAVEL Yup.

NATALYA Oh Pavel I feel sorry for you...

PAVEL You feel sorry for everyone...

NATALYA But we are so alike...

PAVEL You're disabled too? I didn't know.

NATALYA I mean our destinies. We're both clever...

PAVEL You're clever? I didn't know that either...

DUNYA, *wearing a coat, on the way out, is about to enter the room, but hearing the conversation, hides herself.*

NATALYA Don't joke! Your mother thinks I am an idiot so I'm not accepted in this house. I am the wife of the boss but I live like a servant... they don't listen to –

PAVEL Sorry what were you saying?

NATALYA You're the same as me. You have no freedom either.

PAVEL (*Getting more drunk in the warmth.*) Ah but it's all over now! I'll go to town... to Moscow... to everywhere! Screw you all! The house, the land, the lot. I don't want it!

SEMYON *enters, sees* DUNYA, *sneaks up to her, grabs her by the shoulders and howls.*

SEMYON   Aha. Caught you! Spying!

NATALYA   Your mother taught her to.

DUNYA   What are you saying! Spying?! No! I have to –

SEMYON   What were you doing behind the door then?

DUNYA   Please, I have to go –

PAVEL   Hit her in the face till she tells you. You old slump.

DUNYA   I was just... you were talking and I thought I shouldn't disturb you... you think I'd even understand anything?

PAVEL   Don't lie to me!

SEMYON   No. Don't lie to him! He's a master of listening at doors!

PROKHOR *enters,* ANNA *and* LYUDMILA *support him under their arms.*

PROKHOR   Whoa! What's up?!

NATALYA   This one was listening at the door.

LYUDMILA   Let her go Semyon! You all love to torture people!

NATALYA   And you don't?

PROKHOR   Sshh... too loud! No fighting.

SEMYON   We have to think of a punishment for her!

PAVEL   Crush her nose in the door... she won't do it again after that...

LYUDMILA   Tfu! Disgusting!

SEMYON   No no I know! We'll make her drink the oil from
            the icon lamp…

PAVEL   Yes!

ANNA   (*Sternly.*) Leave her alone Semyon! Enough! Go,
            Dunya.

            DUNYA *exits*.

NATALYA   (*To* PAVEL.) It seems we have another boss.

PAVEL   Not for long! None of it will be for long!

SEMYON   Who do you think you are Anna? You don't speak
            to me like that. You don't speak like that to
            anyone in this house.

PROKHOR   Oo – he's woken up at last! Mr Spineless.

PAVEL   Tonight I might release two cats into the pigeon
            loft.

ANNA   Pavel! Don't you dare!

PAVEL   Yes, Semyon's right, who *do* you think you are?

ANNA   Your older sister.

PROKHOR   Let him release what he likes. Release *him*! Let's
            see what happens.

SEMYON   You can't *speak* to us / like that.

NATALYA   Sister with all due respect you're not part of this
            any more.

PAVEL   None of it's going to matter for long!

SEMYON   Natka's right – You got your share – so lie down,
            over there, drink tea, and shut, the fuck, up.

            VASSA *and* MIKHAIL *appear in the doorway*.

PROKHOR   (*To* LYUDMILA.) You all need to think what's
            going to happen in a week's time.

            After forty days –

LYUDMILA	Nothing will happen
PROKHOR	Yes it will! Boof! All gone!
PAVEL	(*To* PROKHOR.) What will happen is that I will send you to hell!
PROKHOR	You twat. I'll…
ANNA	Prokhor! Stop it! Pavel, be careful, if you get him angry he might… well…
PAVEL	What?
PROKHOR	Don't tell him that! He'll do it on purpose!
PAVEL	*What?*
ANNA	(*To* PAVEL.) Just that it's not good for him. The doctor said if he gets too angry he might have a seizure and die.
PROKHOR	Why did you say that?! / Agh…
LYUDMILA	Anna you shouldn't / do this…
PROKHOR	They're doing it on / purpose!
ANNA	Don't get yourself worked up Uncle.
PROKHOR	(*To* ANNA.) Look how she talks, eh? So you're in charge are you?
VASSA	(*Enters*.) She'd certainly like to be.
	Everyone quietens down.
MIKHAIL	(*To* PROKHOR.) How are you Prokhor?
PROKHOR	Ah… asthma… rheumatism… vascular disease, I'm fine!
	SEMYON *laughs.* PAVEL *watches his uncle the whole time.* VASSA *sits.*
VASSA	Semyon did you give orders to take back Klyamzinskii the clerk?
SEMYON	Yes. He's a good man. He drinks a bit I suppose but –

VASSA   So the wife's telling you what to do?

SEMYON   Natalya had nothing to do with it.

VASSA   I meant the clerk's wife.

LYUDMILA   Oo. You let that slip Senya!

PAVEL   You just shut up!

NATALYA   It's not a secret. Yes I did ask Semyon and I'm perfectly entitled to.

PROKHOR   (*Nodding his head.*) Difficult days Vassa! I'm sorry to see them arrive…

VASSA   (*Calmly.*) Thank you Prokhor. Don't forget to feel sorry for yourself.

PROKHOR   (*Maliciously.*) It's going to be tough though isn't it? For you. People these days!

    They used to say that Russians were gentle and kind but look –

NATALYA   I hope you're not calling us wicked? No one here is *wicked*.

LYUDMILA   (*To* ANNA.) What do you think Anna? Are we wicked?

ANNA   I don't know…

LYUDMILA   Because I agree with Natalya – no one here is wicked…

PROKHOR   We-ell, I think you *might* be –

LYUDMILA   (*Heatedly.*) Not wicked just very unhappy. Unhappy, because they don't know how to love.

PAVEL   Lies! I love… I do!

SEMYON   (*To his wife, with a wink.*) J!

LYUDMILA   And no one knows the difference between good and evil –

PROKHOR   Well that is true!

VASSA   (*Threateningly.*) Alright then, fount of all
             knowledge, why don't you tell us then? Tell us
             how to love. How to be good.

MIKHAIL   (*Looking apprehensively at his daughter.*)
             Lyudmila…

LYUDMILA   Your garden is good! I've loved it since I was
             young and when I walk in it now I love you for
             making the earth beautiful…

VASSA   (*Proudly, to* ANNA.) Ah! You hear that?

LYUDMILA   But sometimes I'm scared of you.

MIKHAIL   Lyudmila, don't.

VASSA   Let her continue.

LYUDMILA   Don't worry Father. I look at the garden and
             I remember you with a bent back, digging around
             the apple trees and the berries and the flowers…
             Mumma, you know what's good! You know!
             Nobody else here does…

NATALYA   Well I'm not sure that's / entirely –

SEMYON   Natalya – J!

NATALYA   Shut up!

LYUDMILA   And they never will! Goodness passes them by
             and they'll never see it!

NATALYA   She's a prophet!

PROKHOR   But what does she want?

SEMYON   (*Muttering.*) Anna and her are doing it together.
             They want something from Mum.

VASSA   Semyon keep your thoughts to yourself –

NATALYA   He is not afraid of anyone…

SEMYON   J!

VASSA   Why do you *keep making that stupid fucking
             noise*?

SEMYON   What? J?

PROKHOR   Lyuda – go on, say something else! I'm
              enjoying it.

LYUDMILA   ...No.

VASSA   You don't have to. God bless you with good
              children Lyudmila.

LYUDMILA   (*Indicating her husband.*) From him? Not likely.

MIKHAIL   Lyudmila!

NATALYA   (*Dragging the word out.*) Anyway...

PAVEL   (*Grabbing a knife.*) You're dead!

              VASSA *knocks his elbow, the knife falls out of
              his hand.*

              What are you doing? Saving her?! Then let me
              free! Give me my money! And I'll go!

VASSA   (*Pushing him.*) Shut up!

PAVEL   (*Choking on his words.*) I hate you all...

              Grabbing the candle.

              I'll set fire to you then! Who are you all to me?

              Practically sobbing.

              Are you really my mother? My uncle? My wife?
              Brother? What are any of you to me?

VASSA   (*Threateningly.*) And what are you to all of us?

PAVEL   You're like dogs hunting a hare. Just give me
              what's mine, and I'll go.

VASSA   And what is yours?

NATALYA   What do you mean? All of it! His and Senya's.

ANNA   Natalya shush.

NATALYA   Why?

VASSA	Louse! I told you to shut your fucking mouth!
NATALYA	(*Crying*.) Senya! Why are they / treating me like –
PROKHOR	(*To* ANNA.) I can't take all this, I need to go. Anna, I don't feel well! Where are you?! The shouting!
ANNA	(*Hurriedly going into her mother's room*.) Wait Uncle I'm coming... Mum, with me.

VASSA *goes after her, leaving*.

SEMYON	Mum, you are a disgrace –
PROKHOR	Lyudmila! Come and help me...
VASSA	(*Shouting*.) No. Lyudmila!
ANNA	(*Runs across the dining room*.) Coming Uncle! You see Pavel, he's not well again...
PAVEL	(*Howling*.) I'm in charge here... me, the cripple! Let him die.

ANNA, VASSA *and* LYUDMILA *leave*.

PROKHOR*'s gone purple, leaning on the chair and hissing –*

PROKHOR	V-v-v-agh... Mikhail, take me away... he'll kill me!
PAVEL	(*Jumping in front of him*.) You're right! I will!

General turmoil. NATALYA *wants to take* PROKHOR *out*. MIKHAIL *keeps him on a chair*. SEMYON *grabs his brother by the arm and shouts*.

NATALYA	Pavel... stop it...
MIKHAIL	Please... calm down!...
SEMYON	Leave it! Uncle – get out! Mum they're fighting again!

PAVEL   I've wanted to do this for a long time... ever
               since you... there!

               He hits his uncle in the chest – PROKHOR
               straightens up and kicks him. PAVEL*, gasping,*
               sits on the floor, and PROKHOR *collapses*
               heavily on the chair. ANNA *runs in holding*
               medicine, VASSA *and* LYUDMILA *run out of*
               the study –

               VASSA *rushes towards her son, he is twisting*
               around on the floor, holding his leg –

               ANNA *leans over her uncle.* SEMYON*'s next to*
               his wife. MIKHAIL *takes his daughter by the*
               hand and whispers something to her, his face
               pleading.

SEMYON   (*To his wife.*) Let's get out of here, now –

VASSA   (*To* PAVEL.) How did he hit you...

ANNA   Pavel I told you...

NATALYA   Wait –

PAVEL   Leave me alone!

ANNA   Give him some water...

MIKHAIL   You understand?

LYUDMILA   (*To her father.*) Not now... tell me later –

VASSA   (*Getting up.*) Hot water?

LYUDMILA   Yes, yes... for the heart...

MIKHAIL   We should take him to his room –

LYUDMILA   We can't!

ANNA   Take him... Semyon, help!

NATALYA   (*Watching them vigilantly.*) Don't touch him
               Senya!... I am afraid. They provoked Pavel,
               deliberately... where are you going?

MIKHAIL, ANNA *and* SEMYON *carry out* PROKHOR.

VASSA   What are you hissing about?

NATALYA   We are not servants... we're the owners of all of it.

VASSA   (*Quietly.*) Get out! Get out!

SEMYON returns, PAVEL gets up off the floor, dragging his foot, goes to his mother, holding on to the chair.

NATALYA   Don't shout! Senya – she's shouting at me...

SEMYON   (*Trying to speak authoritatively.*) Mum that's enough! I'm twenty-seven years old, he's twenty-four. . We're adults and that means something, legally! You can't argue with that!

Their mother lifts her glasses to her forehead and stares closely at her sons.

What are you looking at? Well it doesn't matter. Whatever way you look at us, we're in charge. Your sons are your successors. And that's the end of it.

VASSA   (*Calmly, to* PAVEL.) Go and see how your uncle is...

PAVEL   I don't want to... I won't.

SEMYON   Exactly! We'll do what we want!

VASSA   (*Sighing.*) You were born a fool Semyon.

SEMYON   (*Flaring up.*) Stop it! I may be a fool, but according to the law I am the owner!

ANNA   (*Running in.*) Mum. I think Uncle is dead...

Silence.

PAVEL sitting, hiding his head behind the back of the chair.

SEMYON, *unmoving, blinking*. NATALYA
clings to him, shaking.

VASSA *drops her hands and turns to the front
corner of the room, soundlessly moving her lips.*
ANNA, *drumming her fingers on her chest, looks
at her. Shock on* NATALYA*'s face gradually
turns to joy.*

SEMYON   (*Whispering.*) Fucking hell.

NATALYA   (*Also whispering.*) It's ours.

ANNA   (*To both of them.*) Shhh…

VASSA   (*Quietly.*) Well, Pavel, you got you wanted in
the end…

PAVEL   But I… I'm innocent… I'm so pissed, I can't –

SEMYON   Pavel?! What have you done?

VASSA *and* ANNA *exit, but* ANNA *stops in the
doorway.*

NATALYA   (*Gently.*) Pavel, tell us the truth – did they train
you to hit Prokhor?

PASHA   (*Wearily.*) Go away…

SEMYON   (*To his wife.*) What are you getting at?

ANNA   (*Enters.*) Pavel I warned you. I warned you what
might happen.

NATALYA   (*Suspiciously.*) Ye-es… but it looked like you
made him do it –

PAVEL   I'm innocent…

MIKHAIL *enters, his hand wrapped in a
handkerchief,* LYUDMILA *and* VASSA *enter
as well.*

LYUDMILA *goes to the corner, sits there and
cries quietly.*

VASSA   (*Solemnly.*) He's passed.

NATALYA   (*To her husband, in a whisper.*) Look – his hand…

SEMYON   (*Shudders, loudly.*) Where? Whose hand?

VASSA   (*To* NATALYA.) What are you talking about?

NATALYA   I was telling Semyon that Mikhail's hand…

MIKHAIL   (*Hardly concealing his scorn.*) My hand? I caught it in the door, when we were carrying him out. What of it? It doesn't hurt, if that's what you're wondering –

VASSA   Everyone be quiet! Lyudmila, stop! So.

          Pavel? What are we going to do with you?

          Her voice is trembling. She is quiet for a bit, her lips moving.

          Our family doesn't get on. Our filthy linen will be aired in public and dark rumours about us will spread.

PAVEL   Leave me alone…

VASSA   (*Deeper.*) The police might well get involved. As there's money involved.

          Uncle had more than a hundred thousand in our business…

NATALYA   (*Whispering.*) There it is.

SEMYON   (*To his wife, whispering.*) J!

VASSA   People knew that he wanted to take his money out. He told them. And he had no heir, no one to pass it on to. So you see how difficult it all is. You were warned, don't touch him, you will kill him… and you did it anyway.

          Do you understand the crime you've committed?

PAVEL   (*Muttering.*) Enough! Stop torturing me...

He's seen the danger, frightened, jumps, looks at everyone.

You all... my family... no one's talking suddenly.

I don't want to...

What shall I do?

Mum?

Senya?

VASSA   Of course we'll stand by you, in public. But how will you justify yourself before God?

So my advice to you, if this is going to end in any way well for you – is to go to a monastery...

Everyone is shocked. LYUDMILA, *like a blind woman, goes to her mother-in-law and smiles.*

NATALYA   (*To her husband.*) Oh... that's good! You see?

PAVEL   (*Confused.*) I don't want to! What do you mean? Semyon, I don't want to!

VASSA   (*More firmly.*) I'll give them a generous contribution on your behalf, and you'll live there peacefully, innocently, and penitently. You'll become accustomed to worshipping God and you will pray for us every day.

PAVEL   (*In anguish.*) Lyudmila... look... she's happy! Lyuda have pity! Look at me...

Shocked at the look on his wife's face.

So happy... Mumma look who you married me to!

VASSA   You wanted to marry her.

MIKHAIL   (*With difficulty.*) Yes, you did!

VASSA   You remember? You threatened to stab yourself if I stopped you?

NATALYA   Yes! I remember that too…

VASSA   (*Threateningly.*) You be quiet!

Softer, but unshakeable.

So now Pavel, promise me you'll go to the monastery. It'll be better for you and… well, everyone actually. No-one there will laugh at you, no one'll mock you for being… unattractive. And I will have the reassurance that my son is in a peaceful place, and lives in honour.

Have a think… take your time, there's no hurry, in a while you can give me your agreement.

PAVEL   A while?

VASSA   Yes of course.

A few minutes.

PAVEL   (*To his wife.*) You are smiling at my death? I won't forget it.

LYUDMILA   No Pavel, not at your death, at my freedom…

She stands near VASSA, *far from her husband. Not moving from her place, she gets onto her knees.*

Despite everything you're a human being! There must be at least a drop of goodness in you, so let me go Pavel! For Jesus' sake! I'll remember you with kindness – I give you my word I'll think of you with affection in my heart. I might be the only one to think of you like that! Except your mother of course. But I can't stay with you! It hurts me to touch you… especially after today…

Everyone is silent. VASSA *sits, lowers her head.*

Pavel. Pasha! My one. Let me go!

PAVEL   (*Shivers.*) Don't… don't talk like that. Well…

Divorce, maybe. Alright. Why not?

At least we'll know where we stand.

LYUDMILA *gets up, goes to him and kisses him on his forehead without touching him.*

(*Recoils.*) Eurgh! What are you doing? It's like a corpse!

He flares with anger again.

No! I'm not going to a monastery! Let them judge me. The police and everything. You're lying so you can get my money. You're going to give me my money and I'll go to the other end of the earth, and you'll never hear about me again. And maybe I'll be so much more clever than you realise and grow rich, and you will stay here and be poor, and one day you'll come to me on your hands and knees, starving and filthy, diseased and crippled, and you'll beg at my feet for charity, and I will listen carefully, I will smile with kindness, and then I'll kiss you on the fucking head like a corpse and tell my servants to get rid of you and then I'll watch out the window as they beat you all senseless.

Beat.

Give me my money!

VASSA   (*Calmly.*) No.

PAVEL   Give it to me!

NATALYA   (*Agitated.*) But... Vassa... you have to. You've been lording it over us ever since I arrived, like you're better than us, looking down on me, making your jokes about how big I am, whispering after I walk past or when I leave a room. Thinking I'm naive, thinking I'm stupid, but I am not. I am clever, and strong and a much better person than you have ever been. And now your husband is dead and Prokhor is dead and the

business, all of it, and the money it goes to us.
And I finally get to look you in the face and say –

Fuck.

You.

SEMYON   (*Quietly, affectionately.*) It's the law. Mumma.

VASSA   The law?

She smiles.

Have I taught you nothing?

Children make laws. Grown ups make *deals.*

A door is loudly opened, and DUNYA *comes into
the room. She's carrying two copies of the will.
She looks quiet and dishevelled compared to
when we last saw her.*

She walks up to VASSA *and gives her the will.*

DUNYA   The priest said I should deliver this to you.

VASSA   Did you say you had my blessing?

Beat.

DUNYA   He was most grateful.

VASSA   Thank you Dunya.

DUNYA   And he said I should visit again.

VASSA   Then you must.

Beat.

ANNA   Dunya. Are you alright?

She looks at ANNA, *then turns and goes.* ANNA
looks at VASSA, *confused.* VASSA *gives one of
the copies to* MIKHAIL, *and reads the other one.
Then she looks up at the others.*

VASSA   (*Sighing.*) You don't have any inheritance.
Everything has been left to me in the will...

SEMYON   What?! But –

MIKHAIL   That is completely true…

NATALYA   (*To her husband, destroyed.*) It's forged! It must
             be! It's a fake!

VASSA   (*Glancing at her.*) In complete and sole
             ownership.

NATALYA   She's a liar, she's been trying to steal what's ours
             from the moment your father grew ill! –

MIKHAIL   (*Businesslike.*) There were witnesses: Father
             Yegor, Antip Stepanov Mukhoedov, whom you
             know, and also Ryzhev the landowner…

NATALYA   Who *are those people*?!

SEMYON   (*Destroyed.*) Mumma, why are you doing this
             to us?

NATALYA   Show me the paper… where is it?

MIKHAIL   (*Getting the paper.*) The notary has the original,
             but there are two copies – here. One each.

             NATALYA *grabs a copy of the will and reads.*

PAVEL   (*Pushing it away.*) I don't need to see it. I didn't
             really believe my freedom would ever happen,
             you're too cruel for that – so nothing will happen.

             Beat.

             Nothing will happen.

NATALYA   Your own family – even them. What are you?

VASSA   Enough.

             (*To* PAVEL, *quietly.*) Well, Pavel?

PAVEL   (*Looking round.*) You've cornered me.

             Monks don't live in hell I suppose.

             They're still alive.

             Just.

MIKHAIL   (*Reassuringly.*) I promise despite what you hear, they live very well.

PAVEL   (*Mockingly.*) Lyudmila… I know you've already said goodbye, in your own way, but well… out of kindness – give your husband one last kiss.

LYUDMILA   (*Approaching him.*) As long as you don't touch me.

She gets closer. Then suddenly –

PAVEL   Get away from me. Whore. Devil. Slut.

He runs out.

VASSA   (*To* MIKHAIL.) After him! Watch him! Quickly…

MIKHAIL *makes to go.*

MIKHAIL   (*Exiting.*) Do you want me to make an announcement about Prokhor?

VASSA   Yes! It's overdue –

He goes.

SEMYON   (*Dejectedly.*) So, Mother –

VASSA   (*Waving him away.*) Oh go away, go on!

NATALYA   (*Reluctantly bowing low from the waist.*) Mother… forgive me if my words in any way offended –

VASSA   Out. Stop talking and go somewhere else. I can feel I'm about to be incredibly angry with you.

SEMYON *and* NATALYA *exit soundlessly, crushed.* VASSA *gets up, and staggers.*

ANNA   (*Supporting her.*) What? What's the matter.

VASSA   (*Wheezing.*) Cold water… my heart…

LYUDMILA *runs off.*

ANNA   You're exhausted.

VASSA   (*Recovering a little*.) A little tired maybe. It's so difficult.

ANNA   You thought of that so quickly – the monastery…

VASSA   Quickly?! It's taken me years to think of where to deposit him. Miracles just don't exist. Nothing perfect. Nothing given to us. We have to do it all ourselves.

          LYUDMILA *runs in with the water.*

LYUDMILA Here…

          VASSA *drinks the water.*

          God, there's a dead body in the house, and so much grief… but I don't feel anything. It's amazing! Mumma, you're a magician!

VASSA   (*Quietly*.) You're glad?

LYUDMILA I can live all over again! Start from the beginning…

VASSA   Yes. Live with me. I will marry you off. We'll find a good man.

LYUDMILA What?

VASSA   And you can have children, and I will call them my grandchildren… Alright?

LYUDMILA Well I…

VASSA   Because I love you.

LYUDMILA I… I love you too.

VASSA   Good, and you Anna, come and live here, bring your children.

ANNA   My… children…?

VASSA   My son's failed… Yes. Let's try daughters.

          You bring them here. Then we'll see about giving you that contract.

Yes. And the garden will just grow. Your children will run in it. The gentle creatures...

Oh! What? What was that? Hmm?

ANNA   There was no sound.

VASSA   But I heard something... My daughters. Anna I see how you look at me, and yes. I am evil. So many sins. Granted perhaps it was necessary, given the useless individuals I've had to deal with, but even so, I feel sorry for them, now they're defeated.

Still... You love me don't you?... A little bit! I don't ask for much – just a bit! I'm only human...

My son... my little boy...

She jumps, alarmed.

Is he calling?

LYUDMILA   No, there's nothing – what's she talking about?

ANNA   (*Tenderly.*) Everything is quiet... be at peace now...

VASSA   (*Tired.*) I thought...

A moment.

DUNYA *enters. Stands and looks at* VASSA. VASSA *sees her.*

No.

There's no peace for me... there's never any peace...

ANNA *and* LYUDMILA *exchange glances, lean in to* VASSA – *she takes off her glasses, looks at them, smiling gloomily.*

Curtain.